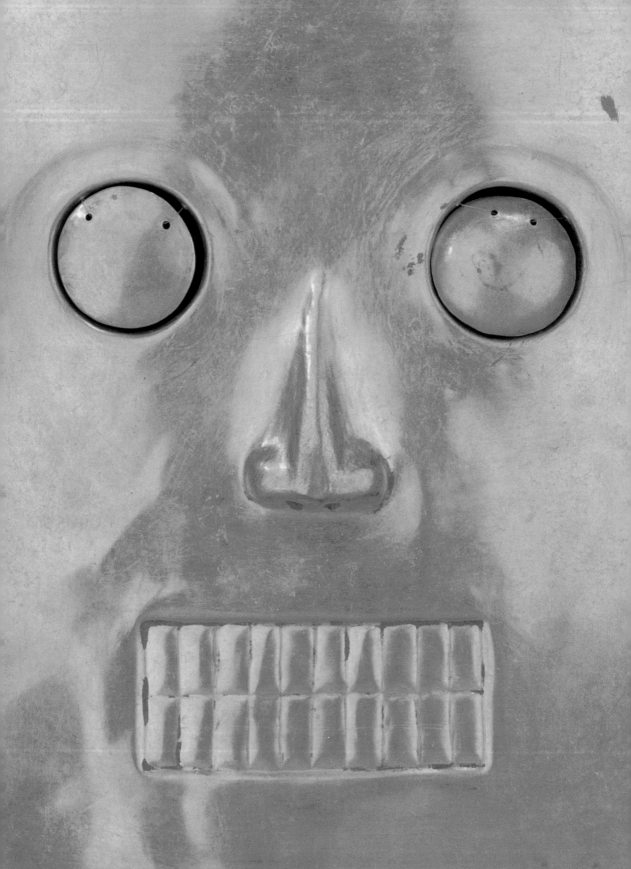

SHAMANS,

GODS,

AND MYTHIC BEASTS:

COLOMBIAN GOLD

AND CERAMICS IN ANTIQUITY

BY

ARMAND J. LABBÉ

FOREWORD BY JULIE JONES

CATALOGUE ENTRIES BY ARMAND J. LABBÉ

ESSAYS BY

WARWICK BRAY, ANA MARÍA FALCHETTI,
LEONOR HERRERA, ARMAND J. LABBÉ,
AND MARIANNE CARDALE SCHRIMPFF

DESIGN BY DOYLE PARTNERS

THE AMERICAN FEDERATION OF ARTS
AND
UNIVERSITY OF WASHINGTON PRESS

THE AMERICAN FEDERATION OF ARTS

is a nonprofit art museum service organization that provides traveling art exhibitions and educational, professional, and technical support programs developed in collaboration with the museum community. Through these programs, the AFA seeks to strengthen the ability of museums to enrich the public's experience and understanding of art.

This catalogue has been published in conjunction with *Shamans, Gods, and Mythic Beasts: Colombian Gold and Ceramics in Antiquity*, an exhibition organized by the American Federation of Arts and the Bowers Museum of Cultural Art. It is a project of ART ACCESS II, a program of the AFA with major support from the Lila Wallace-Reader's Digest Fund. Educational materials are made possible by The Brown Foundation, Inc. Additional support is provided by the Benefactors Circle of the AFA.

Published by The American Federation of Arts, 41 East 65th Street, New York, NY 10021, and University of Washington Press, P.O. Box 50096, Seattle, Washington 98145-5096.

The glossary is adapted from Armand J. Labbé, *Colombia Before Colombus: The People, Culture, and Ceramic Art of Prehispanic Colombia*. New York: Rizzoli International Publications, Inc., 1986.

EXHIBITION ITINERARY

Michael C. Carlos Museum, Emory University
Atlanta, Georgia   October 30, 1998–January 10, 1999

Mingei International Museum of World Folk Art
La Jolla, California   January 29–April 11, 1999

Orlando Museum of Art
Orlando, Florida   April 30–July 11, 1999

The Frick Art Museum
Pittsburgh, Pennsylvania   July 29–October 10, 1999

The Bowers Museum of Cultural Art
Santa Ana, California   October 29, 1999–January 9, 2000

Labbé, Armand J.
    Shamans, gods, and mythic beasts : Colombian gold and ceramics in antiquity/ Armand J. Labbé ; foreword by Julie Jones ; entries by Armand J. Labbé ; essays by Warwick Bray . . . [et al.].
        p.   cm.
    Exhibition itinerary, Michael C. Carlos Museum, Emory University, Atlanta, Ga. Oct. 30, 1998-Jan. 10, 1999 and others.
    Includes bibliographical references and index.
    ISBN 0-295-97755-8
    1. Indian goldwork—Colombia—Exhibitions. 2. Indian sculpture— Colombia— Exhibitions. 3. Indian pottery—Colombia—Exhibitions. 4. Colombia—Antiquities— Exhibitions.   I. Bray, Warwick. II. Michael C. Carlos Museum. III. Title.
    F2270.1.G57L33 1998
    730'.09861'074—dc21
                                                        98-24090
                                                        CIP

Publication Coordinator: Michaelyn Mitchell
Printed in Hong Kong

Front cover: cat. no 146 (detail); Inside front and back cover: map by Daniel Robert Dranger; Page 1: cat. no. 124 (detail); Frontispiece: cat. no. 128 (detail); Page 5: cat. no. 113; Page 6: cat. no. 81; Page 9: cat. no. 20; Page 10: cat. no. 125; Page 13: cat. no. 144; Page 14: cat. no. 40; Page 16: cat. no. 145; Page 19: cat. no. 91; Page 215: cat. no. 76; Page 216: cat. no. 129 (detail).

CONTENTS

LENDERS TO THE EXHIBITION
7

FOREWORD
BY JULIE JONES
7

PREFACE
BY ARMAND J. LABBÉ
9

ACKNOWLEDGMENTS
11

TABLE OF STYLES
15

INTRODUCTION
BY ARMAND J. LABBÉ
17

**SYMBOL, THEME, CONTEXT, AND MEANING
IN THE ART OF PREHISPANIC COLOMBIA**
BY ARMAND J. LABBÉ
21

**THE MALAGANA CHIEFDOM, A NEW
DISCOVERY IN THE CAUCA VALLEY OF
SOUTHWESTERN COLOMBIA**
BY WARWICK BRAY, LEONOR HERRERA, AND
MARIANNE CARDALE SCHRIMPFF
121

**ZENÚ CERAMICS FROM THE
CARIBBEAN LOWLANDS OF COLOMBIA**
BY ANA MARÍA FALCHETTI
163

GLOSSARY
204

REFERENCES
206

PHOTOGRAPH CREDITS
210

INDEX
212

LENDERS TO THE EXHIBITION

THE BOWERS MUSEUM OF CULTURAL ART, SANTA ANA

DALLAS MUSEUM OF ART

DENVER ART MUSEUM

THE FIELD MUSEUM OF NATURAL HISTORY, CHICAGO

FONDO DE PROMOCIÓN DE LA CULTURA,
SANTAFÉ DE BOGOTÁ, COLOMBIA

INSTITUTO COLOMBIANO DE ANTROPOLOGÍA (COLCULTURA),
SANTAFÉ DE BOGOTÁ, COLOMBIA

MICHAEL C. CARLOS MUSEUM, EMORY UNIVERSITY, ATLANTA

MUSEO DEL ORO, BANCO DE LA REPUBLICA,
SANTAFÉ DE BOGOTÁ, COLOMBIA

ANONYMOUS LENDERS

FOREWORD

In the quarter of a century since the American Federation of Arts was first involved in the organization of an exhibition of antiquities from Colombia, much information has been added to the record of the lives and accomplishments of the ancient peoples from the area of northern South America now known as the Republic of Colombia. The previous exhibition, *El Dorado: The Gold of Ancient Colombia,* which was drawn from the impressive holdings of Santafé de Bogotá's Museo del Oro, opened in New York at the Center for Inter-American Relations on Park Avenue in 1974. At that time, the gold objects, which represented the many Colombian goldworking areas, were largely undated and therefore virtually without a conjectural place in the temporal hierarchy of ancient American works.

7.

By contrast, *Shamans, Gods, and Mythic Beasts: Colombian Gold and Ceramics in Antiquity* (also drawn from Colombian collections including the Museo del Oro, as well as other international lenders) presents a substantive time frame within which the works of art can be discussed. There has been considerable research during the last twenty-five years, and Colombian antiquities can now take their appropriate place within the growing awareness of ancient America.

Time frames, or chronologies, are one of the staples of archaeological excavation. When excavating—working from late to early (the proverbial "sterile" soil)—archaeologists build chronologies for specific regions that can be interrelated one to the other, thus providing a structural framework to which information and ideas about peoples, places, and things can be related. Princes, priests, warriors, traders, farmers, hunters, and artisans can be hypothesized and given "flesh" within that framework.

This filling in of the frame comes from the addition to the archaeological record of research into historic archival records and, for comparative purposes, to the study of recent, and relevant, indigenous peoples, their beliefs and their myths. Together, these lead to the formation of hypotheses that allow for the reconstruction of ancient daily life, to projections of social and political rankings, to specialist activities, and to the supposition of esoteric knowledge. Such a structure now exists for ancient Colombia. It is largely the work of Colombian archaeologists, ethnologists, and historians who have made significant advances in understanding the long and productive pre-European era of their country.

JULIE JONES

CURATOR-IN-CHARGE

DEPARTMENT OF THE ARTS OF AFRICA, OCEANIA, AND THE AMERICAS

THE METROPOLITAN MUSEUM OF ART

The earliest works of art in the current exhibition date to the first millennium B.C., and there are those that might date to the preceding millennium. Of course, the latest works are those presumably sixteenth-century pieces that might be from the pivotal time when indigenous life was changed forever with the arrival of the Spaniards in Colombia. Thus for approximately three thousand years, indigenous works of art were produced in northern South America.

Those works of art, not unexpectedly, are particularly characteristic to the time and region of their manufacture. Many of the distinctive types are presented in this exhibition. They include the large, freestanding ceramic figure sculptures of the Tumaco-La Tolita region, with their simplified human depictions and freshness of surface; the right-hand-to-chest bench figures of extreme stylization in ceramic in the Popayán style; the cast gold pendants in Malagana style, with their tight form and complex elaborative detail; and the two-dimensionally rendered Tolima pendants of strong outline and minimal detail.

Many works reflect interaction or understanding within larger spheres of activity, such as pieces that fit into wider American—highland Andean or lowland Caribbean coast—traditions. The spouted ceramic vessels with bodies rendered in sculptural form, or the gold masks considered to be funerary, can find counterparts throughout regions to the west and south in the central Andes; while the double-ended ceramic bowls with wide, elaborated rims point to relationships along the Caribbean coast to the east and south.

Thus, the art of ancient Colombia is both individual in its many varied aspects, and a participant in the larger South American world of its time, factors leading to the diversity of type and complexity of image present in the works of art in *Shamans, Gods, and Mythic Beasts: Colombian Gold and Ceramics in Antiquity.*

PREFACE

The present publication offers the interested scholar and the general public new interpretative perspectives on the prehispanic art of Colombia and exposes the general readership to important new archaeological cultures recently uncovered in southwest and northern Colombia. Chosen from public and private collections in Colombia and the United States, the selections were made on the basis of aesthetic quality, relative rarity, or ethnographic significance. A high percentage of them are unique expressions of prehispanic Colombian art.

Restricting the presentation to archaeologically provenanced examples would have excluded many of the finer works, but the inclusion of unprovenanced works inevitably raises questions of authenticity. It is often impossible to achieve consensus on these points even among experts, and in those cases where questions were raised, each work was meticulously and methodically re-examined. The final responsibility for any and all selections made is my own. The problem of provenance and authenticity only underscores the need for continued controlled excavations, guided by a sensitivity to legitimate indigenous concerns for the preservation of ancestral patrimony. It is only through systematic archaeology that true provenance can be established and cultural context preserved.

Any endeavor such as this could only have resulted from the efforts of numerous individuals. Special thanks are due the heads of the two institutions that organized the exhibition: Serena Rattazzi, director, the American Federation of Arts, and Peter C. Keller, president, the Bowers Museum of Cultural Art. For supporting the project during its initial research stages and lending outstanding works from their respective institutions in Colombia, I want to acknowledge Clara Isabel Botero and Clemencia Plazas, director and former director, respectively, Museo del Oro; Alicia Eugenía Silva, director, Fondo de Promoción de la Cultura; and María Victoria Uribe, director, Instituto Colombiano de Antropología. My appreciation also goes to the representatives of the lending institutions in the United States: at the Dallas Museum of Art, then director Jay Gates, Charles Venable, chief curator, and Carol Robbins, curator of New World and Pacific cultures; at the Denver Art Museum, Lewis I. Sharp, director; at the Field Museum of Natural History, Charles Stannish, associate curator and chair, Department of Anthropology; and at the Michael C. Carlos Museum, Rebecca Stone-Miller, curator of art of the ancient Americas. I am also grateful to the many private collectors in Colombia and the United States who generously agreed to lend their works.

Research and access to the collections were greatly facilitated by Roberto Lleras and Juanita Sáenz Samper at the Museo del Oro; Doris Rojas at the Fondo de Promoción de la Cultura; Kimberly Bush at the Dallas Museum of Art; Laura M. Brannen and Stacey Savatsky at the Michael C. Carlos Museum; Alice Bryant and Jacquie Bryant at the Bowers Museum of Cultural Art; and Diane Rosenblum at the AFA.

For their contributions to the development of the exhibition, I want to thank AFA staff members Thomas Padon, director of exhibitions; Jillian Slonim, director of communications; and Robin Kaye Goodman, exhibitions/publications assistant. Monika Therrien, University of the Andes, Santafé de Bogotá, provided invaluable assistance. At the Bowers Museum I want to acknowledge Janet Baker, director of public programs, Paul Johnson, director of exhibit design and fabrication, and especially Teresa Inga, administrative assistant, division of research and collections, who coordinated research, travel, and communication, developed an artwork database, and supervised a team of interns dedicated to this project. Martha Longenecker, director of the Mingei International Museum, lent important moral support, and archaeologists Warwick Bray, Marianne Cardale Schrimpff, Leonor Herrera, and Ana María Falchetti contributed to the scholarship

ARMAND J. LABBÉ
DIRECTOR
OF RESEARCH AND COLLECTIONS
BOWERS MUSEUM OF CULTURAL ART

of this book. Warwick Bray and Ana María Falchetti also critiqued my essay. I want to acknowledge Robert Sonin for his painstaking review and commentary on the photo captions and text, and Roberto Lleras and Juanita Sáenz Samper of the Museo del Oro for their technical observations. My appreciation goes to Michaelyn Mitchell, head of publications, AFA, whose meticulous attention to detail assured the artistic and scholarly integrity of this book. And lastly, I would like to extend my special thanks to Marie-Thérèse Brincard, senior curator of exhibitions, AFA, who not only oversaw every aspect of the project, but also facilitated the securing of loans and offered constructive advice in the selection of the objects.

10.

ACKNOWLEDGMENTS

The AFA's engagement with the extraordinary arts of ancient Colombia dates to 1974, when it organized with the Center for Inter-American Relations *El Dorado: The Gold of Ancient Colombia*, an exhibition from the collection of the Museo del Oro. *Shamans, Gods, and Mythic Beasts*, borrowed from private collections and eight major museums and drawing upon the considerable research that has been done in this area in the '80s and '90s, is an exciting successor to that important exhibition.

Many people in Colombia and the United States have been involved in the preparation of this project, and we are profoundly grateful to them all. We wish to express particular thanks to Peter C. Keller, president of the Bowers Museum of Cultural Art, the coorganizer of the exhibition; and to Armand J. Labbé, director of research and collections at the Bowers and the curator of the exhibition. Mr. Labbé selected the exhibition and wrote the lead essay and assembled an impressive team of international scholars for the publication. Without Mr. Labbé's dedication and knowledge this exhibition would not have been possible. We want also to express our appreciation to the other contributors to the book: Julie Jones, the Metropolitan Museum of Art; Warwick Bray, University of London Institute of Archaeology; and Colombian archaeologists Ana María Falchetti, Leonor Herrera, and Marianne Cardale Schrimpff.

We want to acknowledge the cooperation and generosity of the lenders to the tour. At the Museo del Oro, this project received initial support from then director Clemencia Plazas, and then from her successor, Clara Isabel Botero, who enthusiastically continued the commitment. At the Fondo de Promoción de la Cultura, Alicia Eugenía Silva, director, was responsible for allowing major pieces from her museum's collection to travel to the United States for the first time for a national tour. María Victoria Uribe, director of the Instituto Colombiano de Antropología, also kindly lent her support to the exhibition. We want to acknowledge the lenders in the United States as well, the Bowers Museum of Cultural Art, the Michael C. Carlos Museum, the Dallas Museum of Art, the Denver Art Museum, and the Field Museum of Natural History. Private collectors in both the United States and Colombia have also been generous in loaning their works.

At the AFA, *Shamans* has benefitted from the skills of numerous staff members, in particular, Marie-Thérèse Brincard, senior curator of exhibitions, who oversaw the organization of this complex exhibition; and Michaelyn Mitchell, head of publications, who supervised the production of this stunning book. Diane Rosenblum, registrar, coordinated all aspects of the intricate handling and packing of the exhibition. Katey Brown, head of education, developed the educational

SERENA RATTAZZI
DIRECTOR
THE AMERICAN FEDERATION OF ARTS

11.

resources. Jillian Slonim, director of communications, guided the promotion and publicity efforts for the project. I also want to recognize Thomas Padon, director of exhibitions; Robin Kaye Goodman, exhibitions/publications assistant; and Priscilla Frost, communications assistant.

We are grateful to Stephen Doyle and Craig Clark of Doyle Partners for their striking design of this publication, to Charles Flowers for his assistance on the editorial side, and to Christian Viveros for his translation of the Spanish texts.

Our special thanks go to Rafael Lamo Gomez, consul general of Colombia in New York, for his support of the project; Monika Therrien, University of the Andes, Santafé de Bogotá, for coordinating the loans from Colombia; and Teresa Inga, administrative assistant to Mr. Labbé at the Bowers Museum of Cultural Art, for invaluable assistance throughout the development of the project.

We want to recognize the museums participating in the national tour of the exhibition: the Bowers Museum of Cultural Art, Santa Ana, California; the Michael C. Carlos Museum, Emory University, Atlanta; the Frick Art Museum, Pittsburgh; the Mingei International Museum of World Folk Art, La Jolla; and the Orlando Museum of Art.

Lastly, we wish to acknowledge the generosity of the Lila Wallace-Reader's Digest Fund, which supported the project through the AFA's ART ACCESS II initiative; the Brown Foundation, Inc.; and the Benefactors Circle of the AFA.

The Fondo de Promoción de la Cultura was created in 1972 as a nonprofit organization dedicated to the conservation and promotion of Colombia's ceramic heritage. Since that time the Fondo has assembled a unique collection of nearly fifteen thousand ceramic objects, many of

ALICIA EUGENÍA SILVA
DIRECTOR
FONDO DE PROMOCIÓN DE LA CULTURA
SANTAFÉ DE BOGOTÁ, COLOMBIA

which are on exhibit at its museums in Santafé de Bogotá (the former home of the Marqués de San Jorge) and in Santiago de Cali (previously the La Merced convent). Both buildings are part of Colombia's architectural heritage and provide excellent historical settings for the collection. In addition to its permanent exhibitions, the Fondo has several thousand ceramic objects in a study collection opened to students and scholars for research and conservation.

The Fondo also organizes exhibitions of ceramics that travel, both within Colombia and abroad. Recent exhibitions have traveled to Guadalajara; Brussels; Seville and Palma de Mallorca in Spain; San Cristobal in Venezuela; Stockholm; Buenos Aires; and Athens. The Fondo produces a wide range of educational materials to accompany these exhibitions. The Fondo has produced "Tierra/Hombre Colombia" (Earth/Man Colombia), for a television series on ancient pottery production intended to promote Colombia's ceramic heritage.

We are grateful for the splendid opportunity that the American Federation of Arts has given the Fondo to present unique pieces from its collection for the first time in North America. We thank the AFA and their staff for the opportunity of collaborating with them in such an important and well-planned traveling exhibition.

CLEMENCIA PLAZAS
FORMER DIRECTOR
AND
CLARA ISABEL BOTERO
DIRECTOR
MUSEO DEL ORO
*SANTAFÉ DE BOGOTÁ,
COLOMBIA*

The Museo del Oro was founded by the Banco de la República in 1939 to promote the importance of Colombian prehispanic gold. Today, the over fifty thousand works in the museum's collection—including pieces in gold, shell, bone, and wood, ceramic and stone objects, and textiles—comprise Colombia's most important group of archaeological material from the ancient Colombian cultures, referred to by archaeologists as Tumaco, Nariño, Calima, Malagana, San Agustín, Tierradentro, Quimbaya, Tolima, Muisca, Sinú, Urabá, and Tairona. Since 1980, the Museo del Oro has opened nine regional museums, each of them specializing in its own local archaeological culture. In addition to circulating thematic exhibitions throughout this network of museums, the Museo del Oro also organizes exhibitions for travel abroad, since 1954 presenting 163 exhibitions in 48 countries.

Shamans, Gods, and Mythic Beasts: Colombian Gold and Ceramics in Antiquity marks the second time the museum and the American Federation of Arts have collaborated to make known to the American public an aspect of Colombia's prehispanic heritage. In 1974, the AFA, together with the Center for Inter-American Relations, organized *El Dorado: The Gold of Ancient Colombia*. Drawn entirely from the collections of the Museo del Oro, the exhibition traveled in the United States and Canada.

We wish to thank the staff of the AFA, in particular Serena Rattazzi, director, and Marie-Thérèse Brincard, senior curator of exhibitions, as well as Peter C. Keller and Armand J. Labbé, president and director of research and collections, respectively, at the Bowers Museum of Cultural Art, for their important contribution to the dissemination of the cultural wealth of the prehispanic past.

13.

TABLE OF STYLES

This table is organized on the basis of styles, which are grouped according to the geographical region or Colombian Department where they are found. The dates given are chronological parameters that mark off the duration of a particular style through time. The styles represent those referenced in the text, and they correspond to similarly named archaeological cultural phases and periods. Unfortunately, our ability to determine the chronological parameters of a particular style is frustrated by a lack of reliable scientifically established dates. Undoubtedly, in the future, additional archaeology and more precise dating techniques will allow us to more accurately date a particular style and to distinguish substyles within a larger stylistic grouping.
—AJL

DEPARTMENT OF NARIÑO

PACIFIC COASTAL REGION
TUMACO-LA TOLITA STYLES CA. 300 B.C.–A.D. 300
HIGHLAND NARIÑO REGION
CAPULÍ STYLE CA. A.D. 850–1500
PIARTAL STYLE CA. A.D. 750–1250
TUZA STYLE CA. A.D. 1250–1500

TIERRADENTRO REGION DATES UNKNOWN

DEPARTMENT OF VALLE DEL CAUCA

CALIMA REGION
ILAMA STYLE CA. 1000 B.C.–A.D. 1
YOTOCO STYLE CA. A.D. 100–800
SONSO STYLE CA. A.D. 800–1600
CAUCA VALLEY REGION
LATE ILAMA STYLE CA. 300–0 B.C.
MALAGANA STYLE CA. 150 B.C.–A.D. 200
POPAYÁN REGION
POPAYÁN STYLE DATES UNKNOWN

MIDDLE CAUCA REGION
CLASSIC QUIMBAYA STYLE (GOLD) CA. A.D. 0–800
BROWN INCISED STYLE CA. A.D. 500–800
LATE QUIMBAYA STYLE CA. A.D. 800–1600
MIDDLE SINÚ RIVER REGION
BETANCÍ MODELED-AND-INCISED STYLE
CA. A.D. 1000–1500
MIDDLE AND LOWER SAN JORGE RIVER REGION
MONTELIBANO STYLE CA. A.D. 800–1000
EARLY ZENÚ GOLDWORK GROUP DATES UNKNOWN
CARIBBEAN LOWLAND REGION DATES UNKNOWN
GULF OF URABÁ REGION
GULF OF URABÁ REGIONAL STYLES DATES UNKNOWN
TAIRONA REGION
MALAMBOID STYLE CA. 1100–100 B.C.
NAGUANJE STYLE CA. A.D. 200–900
TAIRONA STYLE CA. A.D. 800–1600
LATE TAIRONA STYLE CA. A.D. 1000–1600
DEPARTMENT OF MAGDALENA
CHIMILA STYLE DATES UNKNOWN
BAJA GUAJIRA REGION
RANCHERÍA STYLE 500 B.C.–A.D. 1000
MUISCA REGION
HERRERA STYLE CA. 1300 B.C.–A.D. 900
MUISCA STYLE CA. A.D. 900–1600

MAGDALENA RIVER REGION

LOWER MAGDALENA RIVER REGION
MALAMBO STYLE CA. 1100–100 B.C.
MALIBÚ STYLE A.D. 1300–1700
MOSKITO STYLE CA. A.D. 1000–1500
PELAYA STYLE CA. A.D. 1000–1500
TAMALAMEQUE STYLE CA. A.D. 800–1500
MIDDLE MAGDALENA RIVER REGION
EARLY TOLIMA STYLE A.D. 200–1000
TOLIMA STYLE CA. A.D. 200–1600
PUBENZA POLYCHROME STYLE CA. A.D. 1000–1400

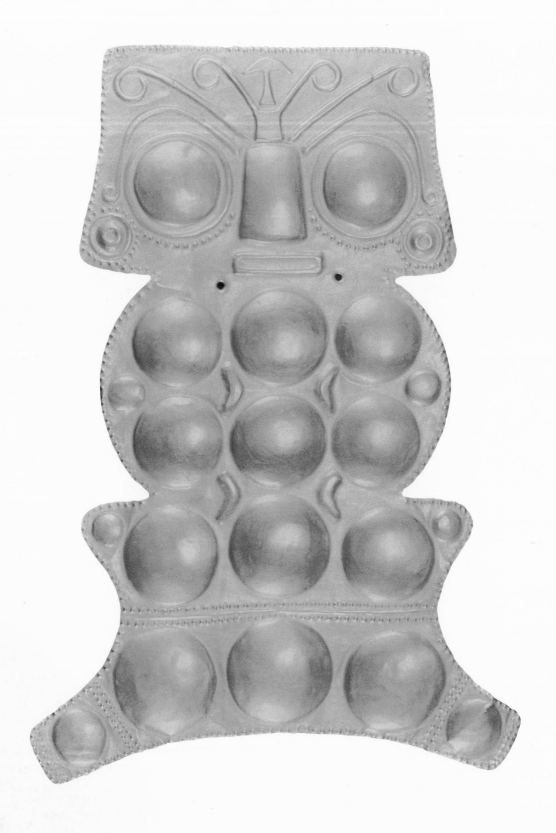

INTRODUCTION

BY
ARMAND J.
LABBÉ

In prehistoric times Colombia was the crossroads of the Americas and a melting pot of cultures and ethnicities. Recent archaeological discoveries have established northern Colombia as one of the earliest ceramic producing areas of the New World. How these cultures developed, where they originated, and how they came to be dispersed are questions we can only partially answer. Some answers can be found in an understanding of Colombia's topography.

Three rugged mountain chains—the Eastern, Central, and Western Cordilleras—divide the country longitudinally. Running the length of the Cordilleras in the great valleys below are two of the country's main rivers—the Magdalena, which flows between the Eastern and Central Cordilleras, and the Cauca, which courses between the Central and Western Cordilleras. Each Cordillera harbors innumerable small valleys that branch eastward or westward off the main spine of each mountain chain.

The Pacific Coast of Colombia receives some of the highest annual rainfall recorded anywhere in the world—up to thirty feet per year—and much of the northern part of the country is a broad floodplain subject to annual flooding. To the east of the Eastern Cordillera lie areas dominated by large river drainage systems. These lush wet environments, which contrast sharply with the arid desert-like conditions of the extreme northeastern region known as La Guajira, do not promote the preservation of ancient artifacts.

Colombia's topography favored political independence and cultural diversity. Even the Inca, who sought to expand their empire into Colombia from their bases in Ecuador, were thwarted as much by the rigors of the Colombian landscape as they were by the resolute resistance they met from Colombia's independent-minded Indians. Nonetheless, in the era just before the Spanish conquest large federated chiefdoms had formed both in the northern areas dominated by the Tairona culture and in the savannas of the Eastern Cordillera, home to the Muisca and Guane Indians.

The reconstruction of Colombia's pre-Columbian past is a relatively recent endeavor involving archaeologists, anthropologists, ethnographers, and historians. With most of the significant work in these areas having been undertaken within the last fifty years, the task of developing an art history for the prehispanic eras is still in its infancy.

This publication seeks to document and interpret the artistic themes and iconography of some of the civilized cultures that flourished in Colombia prior to the Spanish conquest. The interpretations presented here are not fixed but rather constitute a continuing story of ever-increasing awareness.

The prehispanic ceramics and goldworks reproduced in this volume serve to document an important cognitive dimension of culture relevant to indigenous religion, myth, cosmology, and sociology. These objects are presented not only as chronological and typological index markers of specific cultures, or as documents illustrating some of the basic ideas developed in the text, but also as fine art. Pre-Columbian art is, however, almost never simply art for art's sake. More often than not it reflects cultural myth and ideology encoded in metaphor and symbolism.

In order to understand this art we must transcend mere aesthetic appreciation or personal aesthetic bias and reintegrate it within its cultural milieu. Traditional Colombian Indian values and perceptions of how the world is organized differ markedly from those of contemporary western civilization. Where we emphasize individual lives and egos, they emphasize life. Where we create celebrities, they celebrate nature. Both the Kogi priest of the Sierra Nevada de Santa Marta and his Hopi counterpart on the mesas of northern Arizona in North America perceive themselves as guardians of fertility and custodians of the biosphere whereas the will of western man is set against the play of nature. For the westerner nature is something apart, to be dominated, tamed, controlled, or exploited. For the traditional Indian, it is impossible to conceive of man as separate from nature. In addition, he sees the human community as not only part of the natural order but also part of a greater aggregate. This aggregate includes the visible biosphere and additionally and inseparably that which we in the West normally conceive of either as death, a final end, or a spiritual realm distinct and apart. Death for the Indian, however, is a process of transformation. It is not a separate and distinct state but part of the same process that generates life itself. Out of death comes new life. Superficially, the Indian is empirically reminded of this belief in everyday life. Plants and animals die, decompose, and serve as the building material of new forms. To ascertain the truth or fallacy of other realms of existence, the Indian depends on the guidance of a shaman.

In the prehispanic art of Colombia there are no statues representing great generals, scientists, or statesmen. Culture heroes like Bochica and Bachue of the Muisca are personifications of natural forces rather than representations of specific individuals. This is not to deny the role or reality of ego in native cultures, only to emphasize that it is not reflected in art and is subordinate to nature in the psychological perspective of the traditional Indian.

Our interpretations of artworks are, whenever possible, based on indigenous Colombian ethnographic data. Occasionally, references are made to groups from Mesoamerica or to native groups from the American Southwest such as the Pueblo Indians. The author's research in those areas has convinced him that underlying many apparent differences in culture from one group to another are cognitive similarities and cultural homologies. In this respect it is noteworthy that the ancient civilized cultures of the American Southwest were essentially the most northerly recipients of the great technological and cultural traditions that originated in Meso- and South America. In fact, within the vast area embracing the American Southwest, Mexico, Central America, and northern and western South America, most of the lines of cultural diffusion indicate points of origination from the south. Ceramic production, metallurgy, textile making, and other civilized cultural traits all occur earlier in South America than they do in North America. The evidence suggests that many other important plant domesticates—such as manioc, pineapple, achiote, chontaduro, and cacao—originated in South America and spread northward to Central and Mesoamerica.

Diffusion persists over time and once set in motion is not restricted to any one direction or area. If technologies spread readily from South America to North America, it should not be surprising to find commonalities in other aspects of culture such as mythic belief and ideas. Ideological similarities are not always apparent, however, for they are often disguised in metaphor that may conceal their true identity.

The three essays that follow reflect distinct scholarly perspectives. The first essay focuses on cultural themes and symbolism portrayed in the pre-Columbian art of Colombia. Next, Bray, Cardale Schrimpff, and Herrera's essay reflects the perspectives of three archaeologists on the artistic significance and archaeological context of the recently discovered Malagana-style artifacts from the Cauca Valley of Southwestern Colombia. Finally, Ana María Falchetti's essay explores the relationship of the gold and ceramic art of the Sinú region to concepts of gender, status, and socio-cultural organization.

SYMBOL, THEME, CONTEXT,

AND MEANING

IN THE ART OF PREHISPANIC COLOMBIA

by Armand J. Labbé

PRE-COLUMBIAN

art is richly symbolic. Each element in an artistic composition is typically full of meaning. Color may be coded to reflect gender. Straight lines may be contrasted with curved lines to represent gender or other paired categories. Body ornaments like earspools, nose rings, labrets, and pectorals indicate status while their specific form or design may reflect an individual's ethnic or regional affiliations or identify his or her social function. Posture is also significant.

In the art of Colombia, however, determining whether a figure is standing or seated is not always a simple matter. The artists loved abstraction and stylization, often preferring to suggest and imply rather than depict and define. Slits representing eyes and mouth are sometimes our only clues that a human face is intended. In certain pottery representations of figures seated on a bench that have been

FIGURE SEATED ON A BENCH

I.

The crisp contours of the sculpting and the open mouth with square teeth are characteristic of the Malagana style, although the use of three colors is not. The posture, unusual for figures seated on a bench, may be a shamanic stance used to induce the altered state of consciousness suggested by the intense facial expression and erect phallus. Erect phalli are often associated with figures chewing coca leaf and may have been used as a symbol of empowerment. Department of Valle del Cauca. Malagana style. Ca. 150 B.C.-A.D. 200. Tan pottery with red slip and white details. 10¼" h. x 6⅜" w. Private collection. Publications: Rojas de Perdomo 1995; Archila 1996, pl. 58.

found in the Middle Cauca region, the bench is not readily apparent. It is formed by extending the slab-shaped body (cat. no. 15) so that the extension serves as the bench. The seated posture is implied by tubular legs bent at the knees and tubular hands resting on the knees, artistic conventions used in Colombia to depict a definitive form of seated posture.

Representations of the human form are usually generic and characterized by stylistic conventions used to represent details of face or limb. These conventions can vary by style and region, but some are part of the stock artistic inventory, whatever the group or place of origin. For example, shamans, priests, and rulers are portrayed as generic types, not specific individuals. Deities, though portrayed in human form, are distinguished by a combination of symbolic elements. This emphasis on generic representation and stylistic convention derives from cultural perspectives that tend to de-emphasize the significance of individual ego in favor of social and communal ideals.

Research over the last thirty years has slowly penetrated some of the rich hidden meaning enshrined in the imagery of the prehispanic art of the Americas. The general public has become aware of these advances in regard to such cultures as the Olmec, Maya, and Aztec of Mesoamerica and the Moche of Peru. Unfortunately, the equally fascinating cultures of the so-called Intermediate Area, which includes lower Central America, Colombia, and Ecuador, are less widely known.

The rich symbolic imagery of the prehispanic art of Colombia holds great promise for increasing our understanding of the ethnographic past. There has been great progress in deciphering iconography but little in identifying the themes portrayed or their cultural relevance. It would seem fruitful, therefore, to reexamine the pre-Columbian art of Colombia from a thematic point of view in order to distinguish that which is widespread from that which is unique. This approach should help identify the underlying laws, patterns, and relationships that governed the creation of these works. It should also aid in understanding the role of pre-Columbian art in communicating shared ideas about man, the cosmos, and the human condition.

Some themes are restricted to particular cultures of Colombia, but others, like the "figure seated on a bench" theme, are found in almost every region. The stylistic and iconographic differences and similarities of such widespread themes will be examined and compared on a regional basis.

The themes are portrayed in a number of mediums—clay, metal, stone, wood, shell, and textiles. It is the body of artworks made from clay or gold, however, that offers the largest resource and the broadest range and widest variety of portrayals.

MALE FIGURE SEATED ON A BENCH

In the Tumaco-La Tolita style great emphasis is given to the proportions and details of face and head while the arms, trunk, and legs are rendered more perfunctorily. The bench, necklace, armbands, and legbands emphasize the elevated status of the seated figure. Gold rings or other ornaments may have been attached to the holes at the ears and nose sceptum. Pacific Coastal region, Department of Nariño. Tumaco-La Tolita style. 300 B.C.-A.D. 300. Grey-white pottery. 15" h. x 8¾" w. Fondo de Promoción de la Cultura (T-08846). Publications: Bray 1978, no. 514; *Arte de la Tierra, Colombia: Tumaco* 1994; *Arte de la Tierra, Colombia: Poder* 1994, no. 6.; *Arte de la Tierra, Colombia: Forma y Figura* 1992, cover.

2.

4. & 5.

NECKLACE AND LIME FLASK (POPORO)

The necklace is composed of a series of hollow gold beads of various sizes. Middle Cauca region. Classic Quimbaya style. Ca. A.D. 0-800. Gold. 1 1/16" l. each bead. Museo del Oro (328)

Poporos are containers that hold the lime used in coca-leaf chewing. The lime flasks are often equipped with a small stick or dipper, which is moistened in the mouth, dipped in the lime, and then chewed to assist in extracting the coca alkaloids from the leaves. *Poporos* continue to be used by indigenous groups such as the Kogi and Ika of the Sierra Nevada de Santa Marta in northern Colombia. Middle Cauca region. Classic Quimbaya style. Ca. A.D. 0-800. Cast gold. 4 3/8" h. x 3 3/4" w. (flask only). Museo del Oro (338)

FIGURE SEATED ON A BENCH

3.

The long ribbonlike arms and appliquéd fillets used for the eyes and mouth are typical of the Muisca style. The large staff with opposing spirals identifies the seated figure as a ruler, priest, or shaman. Muisca region. Muisca style. Ca. A.D. 900-1600. Gold. 1 7/8" h. x 7/8" w. Museo del Oro (6780). Publications: Reichel-Dolmatoff 1988, no. 14.

The seated posture is the most common portrayal

of the human form in the art of prehispanic Colombia. Seated figures are usually distinguished by gender, as well as by the positioning and placement of hands and feet. Generally speaking, female seated figures are portrayed seated on the ground while male figures usually sit on a bench. Catalogue number 35, a male companion piece to a standing female figure (cat. no. 51), is an unusual example of gender role reversal. The male is seated on the ground while the female stands upright.

fig. I

CANASTERO ON BENCH
Calima region. Ilama style.
Ca. 1000 B.C.-A.D. 1
Pottery with red-brown slip.
Private collection.
Drawing by Joseph Kramer.

In certain representations, such as the *canastero* genre, gender is not always clearly indicated, and the bench, if intended, is not depicted but implied. *Canastero*, meaning "basket-maker" or "basket-carrier," is a popular term used for a specific type of anthropomorphic vessel characterized by a human figure with an open receptacle at the back. It is unlikely that these figures actually represent merchants with large carrying baskets for their goods. The receptacle at the back of the figure likely had another, though unknown, meaning. The seated posture is sometimes implied by the positioning of the hands on the knees. In a few examples (cat. no. 19), the arms are crossed and resting on the knees. If the upper and lower leg are articulated to form a 90-degree angle, a bench is implied. If the angle is less than 70 degrees a squatting posture is probably intended.

The majority of seated female figures, particularly those from the Middle Cauca region and Highland Nariño, are companion pieces to male figures seated on a bench found in funerary contexts. In such cases, the female figure sits on the ground with legs extended.

In some regions, most notably the Baja Guajira (cat. no. 36), seated females have splayed legs and stylized arms shaped like lugs. This composition suggests an emphasis on the procreative power of women.

In the Muisca region, as elsewhere, both male and female figures are found in seated posture (cat. nos. 32, 33). They are invariably either depictions of dignitaries—that is, individuals of high social status such as rulers or priests—or else anthropomorphic deities like the culture hero Bochica, who taught mankind the arts and sciences, or the goddess Bachue, the mother of mankind. The bench is rarely depicted realistically in the ceramic art of the Muisca. Indeed, it is impossible in most cases to determine whether or not a bench is implied in the composition, regardless of the gender of the figure.

The problem is further complicated for certain ceramic figures from the Sinú and Gulf of Urabá regions. Sometimes it is even difficult to determine whether the figure is standing or seated. For example, a female figure from the Gulf of Urabá (cat. no. 18) appears at first glance to be standing upright. On closer examination, however, it becomes apparent that the knees are bent and the lower legs are at right angles to the full ample thighs. The hands, which initially look as if they are resting on the hips, implying a standing posture, are actually placed on the thighs. The figure is smiling and composed. There is no indication of discomfort or stress. Without some kind of material support such as a bench, however, this seated position would be difficult to sustain without physical discomfort. Hence, it seems reasonable to assume that a bench or support is implied.

In another example, which is in a Malibú-related style (cat. no. 17), the stem of the vessel is anthropomorphized. The figure's body is indistinguishable from the stem. Although the legs and feet are so abstracted as to be barely discernible, the hands are clearly positioned frontally and placed above and atop the knees. This and the serene demeanor of the face suggest the seated posture associated with the bench in realistic portrayals found throughout Colombia. This artwork and similar examples must be viewed against the backdrop of artistic canons, stylistic conventions, and iconographic context crafted and determined by the prehistoric peoples.

Even today, the bench is an important cultural icon among Colombia's indigenous peoples. Usually the prerogative of adult initiated males, the bench is also closely associated with shamans and leaders, symbolizing both shamanic trance and secular authority.

Although the bench theme is widespread throughout prehispanic Colombia, its depiction is nonetheless relatively rare. Because the majority of surviving pre-Columbian artworks in Colombia originated as tomb sculpture to be buried with the deceased, we may conclude that such figures were interred only with certain individuals, possibly chieftains, shamans, or priests. A possible exception is the *retablo*, or slab figure, of the Middle Cauca River region, that portrays a figure seated on a bench in abstract form. These funerary

FEMALE FIGURE SEATED ON A BENCH (FOLLOWING PAGES)

By pulling back the powerful shoulders the artist has given added emphasis to the pregnant lower abdomen. Females seated on benches are rare but not unknown in the art of prehispanic Colombia. In the context of Tairona art such figures are probably reflective of contact between lowland groups and groups along the Lower Rio Magdalena and further afield in the Middle Sinú region, where the depiction of female dignitaries seated on stools is occasionally found. The minimal decoration applied to the figure is also unusual. Typically, Tairona figures seated on a bench are male and are ornately decorated. Minca, Tairona region. Late Tairona style. Ca. A.D. 1000-1600. Black pottery. 11 ½" h. Museo del Oro (CT2292). Publications: Bray 1978, no. 328.

6.

FIGURE SEATED ON A BENCH (FOLLOWING PAGES)

There are few Tairona ceramic sculptures as large as this example. The face and the distended tongue are typically Tairona. This sculpture represents a priest or a shaman in ritual pose. It is unclear whether the two serpents the figure is holding are serpent scepters or forces emanating from his body. The same is true of the serpents seen atop his head, which may be part of a headdress or may signify emanations. Such emanations are associated with empowered shamans and are called *tingunas* by certain groups in the Peruvian Amazon. The symbolic significance of the distended tongue, a stock icon in the art of the Tairona, is uncertain. In Mesoamerica the extended tongue is associated with the sun as life-giver. In part, it signifies self-sacrifice. Among the Tlingit Indians of Alaska a distended tongue is indicative of shamanic trance. In pre-Columbian art the serpent is often used as a symbol of the life force that animates all living things. Sun rays are sometimes graphically represented as undulating serpents and are perceived as the semen of the sun and seeds of life. Among many Colombian groups the sun is considered First Shaman, and all human shamans are no more than apprentices and disciples of the sun. Tairona region. Late Tairona style. Ca. A.D. 1000-1600. Grey-brown pottery. 13⅝" h. x 12⅝" w. Museo del Oro (CT736)

7.

FEMALE FIGURE SEATED ON A BENCH

FIGURE SEATED ON A BENCH

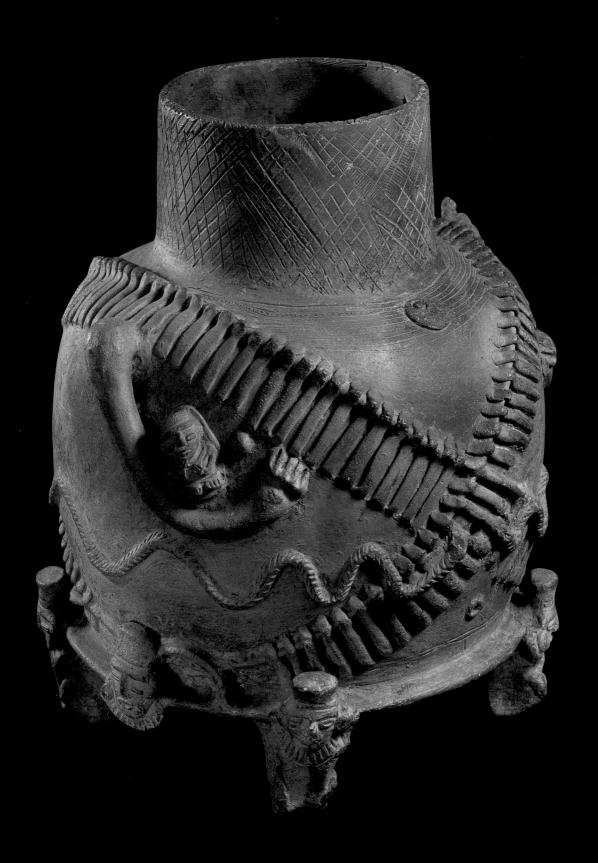

figures are more abundant and found in larger concentrations than variants uncovered in other parts of Colombia.

It is difficult to determine when the figure-seated-on-a-bench theme first appeared because we lack firm dates with which to establish the time frames of particular styles within a culture. For example, a figure seated on a bench in a general Tumaco style, from the Pacific Coast of the Department of Nariño or adjacent areas in Ecuador, presents us with a daunting thousand-year-long continuity of this style. The same challenge holds for the Ilama style of the Calima region. Recognizing where within the millennium a particular artwork falls requires distinguishing and dating substyles within a larger grouping.

The earliest Colombian example of a ceramic artwork incorporating a bench, as well as a figure, was found in the Calima region (fig. 1), a rich, fertile land embracing the upper Calima Valley and surrounding areas of the Cordillera Occidental. Three major distinct ceramic styles have been identified within this region—the Ilama (ca. 1000 B.C.–A.D. 1), the Yotoco (ca. A.D. 0–800), and the Sonso (ca. A.D. 800–1600). In addition, the Malagana style of the Cauca Valley, the subject of another essay within this volume, appears to have very close affinities to the general Yotoco style. Figures on a bench are extremely rare in any of these styles.

The earliest example known is in the Ilama style and probably dates to the middle of the Ilama chronological sequence, somewhere between 600 and 400 B.C. The problem with this piece (fig. 1; Cardale Schrimpff et al. 1991, 33, pl. 23) is the ambiguity in the composition, which portrays a naked male *canastero* squatting on a bench. But, atypically, the lower legs and feet are positioned atop the bench. In orthodox compositions the legs hang over the edge of the bench and the feet touch the ground. Here, the *canastero* squats with hands on knees, a stance typical of Ilama portrayals. It is the combination of bench and *canastero* that is unusual. The composition may be a theme taken from Ilama mythology or allegory rather than a realistic portrayal. This piece is exceptional, if not unique. Since similar portrayals are unknown, we may conclude that figures seated on a bench did not constitute an important genre for the Ilama artists.

In fact, the earliest unambiguous portrayal within the Calima and Cauca

DIGNITARY SEATED ON A BENCH

8.

The foreshortened fillets of clay used as the arms and legs of the central figure are typical of the Muisca style. The contrast between his large body and the diminutive assistant figures underscores the mythical or supernatural nature of the central figure. The massiveness of the body and the lack of face call attention to the power of the individual rather than to personality. The crossed bands are composed of abstract animal pendants, possibly birds, that replicate similar actual pendants found in Muisca goldwork. Bird pendants are closely associated with shamanic concepts. The smaller humanlike figures are depicted assisting the central figure by serving as supports for the bench. The two serpents encircling the body and facing one another at the navel are possibly an allusion to the binary nature (male-female) of life, on which pre-Columbian peoples placed great emphasis. One reason for using the serpent as a symbol of the life force was that the serpent's tongue was split, thereby underscoring the perception that every phenomenon results from the interaction and union of both male and female aspects of an underlying essence. Muisca region. Muisca style. Ca. A.D. 1000-1600. Pottery. 13⅜" h. x 12" w. Fondo de Promoción de la Cultura (M00977). Publications: *Arte de la Tierra, Colombia: Poder* 1994, no. 8; *Arte de la Tierra* 1989, no. 55 and cover.

31.

Valley regions is an *alcarraza* rendered in the Malagana style (cat. no. 1), but the hands are uncharacteristically held aloft, touching the sides of the head. The composition is unique and exceptional and begs interpretation as much as it informs.

Figures seated on a bench or stool form recurrent themes within the art of Tumaco-La Tolita. The Tumaco region, located along the southern Pacific Coast of Colombia in the Department of Nariño, is the northern extension of a culture zone that ran southward along the coast of Ecuador. The Ecuadorian manifestation of this culture is called La Tolita.

The most common portrayal is that of an elite personage—a ruler, priest, or shaman—seated on a four-legged rectangular bench (cat. no. 2). Impassive, the figure imparts a sense of inner calm and contemplation as the hands rest on the knees. Both posture and facial demeanor are hallmarks of the theme in its most orthodox and widespread form within Colombia. Most Tumaco-La Tolita portrayals are large by Colombian prehispanic standards, measuring twelve to fifteen inches or more in height.

There are a number of variants in the Tumaco-La Tolita style. In the most common, the head glances to the right or left rather than facing forward. Since the arms are generally missing in surviving specimens, it is unclear whether the hands were positioned on the knees. Typically, the figure's genitalia are either not depicted or have been lost. If one judges gender by the appearance of the breasts, however, then the majority of depictions represent males.

Seated females are depicted in a variety of poses. The most common have one arm laid across the lap, with the other supporting the jaw, recalling Rodin's *Thinker*. In another variant, the figure holds hands to breasts as if to emphasize her maternal role as nourisher. These females are seated on round stools, however, rather than on rectangular benches. Interestingly, none of the figures seated on stools are portrayed with hands placed on knees, an important iconographic convention in portrayals of male authority figures.

The Middle Cauca region lies to the north of the Calima Zone and includes the Middle Cauca River valley and adjacent slopes and mountains of the modern departments of Quindio, Risaralda, Caldas, and the southern portion of the Department of Antioquía. The earliest figures seated on a bench in the Middle Cauca region were cast in gold in the Classic Quimbaya style, believed to date between A.D. 0 and 800. Usually hollow cast flasks

OCARINA: SEATED DIGNITARY

Ceramic *ocarinas* in the form of a winged figure are peculiar to the Tairona culture. The incised decoration is highlighted by a white substance, the use of which may have had symbolic significance. The image of an anthropomorphic winged figure likely represents a shaman in "soul flight." Shamans were believed capable of leaving their bodies to fly about from place to place, including interdimensional travel to the "Upper World" and "Lower World." Winged anthropomorphic personages are found over wide areas of South and Central America and are depicted in both the graphic and plastic arts. Tairona region. Late Tairona style. Ca. A.D. 1000-1600. Black pottery. 3⅜" h. x 3⅛" w. Private collection

9.

EARSPOOLS

Although these earspools were found in the Gulf of Urabá region, they are stylistically identical to those seen on a seated male figure in Malagana style from the Cauca Valley (cat. no. 1). Gulf of Urabá region. Gulf of Urabá regional style. Date unknown. Gold. 1⅛" h. x ⅞" w. and 1⅛" h. x ⅞" w. Museo del Oro (33478 and 33479)

10.

12.

FIGURE SEATED ON A BENCH

The basic jar form has been only slightly modified to depict a figure seated on a bench. This design incorporates crosshatching, punctating, and incising. The figure combines human and animal characteristics. The fine elaborate crosshatching of the upper body gives the figure the appearance of having snake or lizardlike skin. The posture and arms, however, are characteristically human. The head and face are human but with distorted proportions. The tongue is split in two with a deeply incised median line. Tairona region. Late Tairona style. Ca. A.D. 1000-1600. Black pottery. 2⅛" h. x 2¼" w. Private collection

FUNERARY URN: MALE SEATED ON A BENCH

Moskito-style burial urns are typified by solitary full-bodied figures seated either on benches or lids. Also customary are depressions on the legs caused by ligatures. Highly elaborate funerary urns such as this were used in secondary burial rites in which the bones of the deceased were collected and placed in ceramic urns that were buried in shaft graves located in well-defined burial complexes. Remains of paint are rarely found on burial urns from the Lower Magdalena River. Lower Magdalena River region. Moskito style. A.D. 1000-1500. Buff pottery with white and black paint. 37" h. x 14⅜" w. Museo del Oro (Cmos-786)

11.

13.

OCARINA: SEATED DIGNITARY

In the figural art of the Tairona the image of a dignitary seated on a double-headed dragon bench is a stock theme closely associated with ceramic *ocarinas*, multitonal musical instruments. Shown wearing an elaborate headdress, the central figure most likely represents the solar deity seated on his double-headed dragon bench, an image still used by the Kogi Indians in their mythology.

At the base of the headdress is a band of complementary inverted triangles symbolizing fertility. Similar bands are seen on the figures in the Malagana style of the Calima region. The headdress itself appears to represent rays emanating from the head of the solar deity. In actual ritual these may have been symbolized by feathers. Framing the "rays" is a band containing two rows of dots. Dots were commonly used in pre-Columbian art to represent seeds, potential new life. Indians throughout the Americas viewed the sun as the source of life. The Aztecs of Mexico called the rays of the sun Xiucoatl or "fire-serpents," the life-giving "semen" of the sun.

In Mesoamerican iconography the long split distended tongue is also associated with the sun. Tairona region. Late Tairona style. Ca. A.D. 1000-1600. Brown pottery. 3½" h. x 3⅜" w. Private collection. Publications: Labbé 1986, pl. 59; Labbé 1988, pl. 59.

incorporating a dignitary seated on a bench, these flasks, known as *poporos*, were used as receptacles for the lime used in chewing coca leaf. The earliest ceramic examples date between A.D. 800 and 1200. They are executed in a style referred to as Late Quimbaya, although there is no established ethnic or cultural relationship between the peoples responsible for these artworks and those called Classic Quimbaya.

Figures in the Late Quimbaya style fall into a number of substyles, ranging from stylized realism in which both the human figure and the bench are readily identifiable (*Arte de la Tierra* 1990, nos. 41, 65) to stylized abstractions. The latter are characterized by "cubist" expressions of the human form and benches that are extensions of the slab construction used to fashion the body (cat. no. 15).

This cubist substyle is characterized by two types—solid slab-constructed compositions popularly known as *retablos*; and hollow body figures rendered in the same style. The most common composition is a single figure seated on a bench with the hands placed on the knees. It is often difficult to determine gender, but where it is possible, the majority are males. The companion female figures lack benches and are portrayed seated directly on the ground. There are notable exceptions, however. A figure in the collection of the Banco Popular, Fondo de Promoción de la Cultura, in Santafé de Bogotá (*Arte de la Tierra* 1990, no. 70), an example of the hollow cubist style, is female. It is identical in virtually every respect to the male form except that female genitalia are indicated.

Variants of the theme are mainly distinguished by the positioning of arms and hands. In some specimens the arms are bent at the elbow while forearms extend forward with palms open upward (*Arte de la Tierra* 1990, no. 79; Labbé 1986, pl. 20). In others, the hands are held inward at the chest. In yet other cases, the arm is extended outward with hand raised palm up. Obviously, each of these gestures held specific meaning. It is unfortunate that there is nothing analogous in today's indigenous cultures to guide an interpretation of the symbolic meaning of these pre-Columbian gestures.

Figures seated on a bench are rare in the art of the Sinú and San Jorge River drainages, a broad floodplain characterized by grassy lowlands only occasionally broken by lonely highland outcrops. The area is crossed by important rivers including the San Jorge, Sinú, and Nechi, along which a number of significant cultures flourished and waned. Most of the rare surviving examples are in Betancí style (Labbé 1986, no. 92). Gender is often difficult to identify, but the majority appear to be female. This is not entirely surprising since female figures

BURIAL URN: FIGURE SEATED ON A BENCH

The burial urns of the Middle Magdalena differ from those of the Lower Magdalena River in that the base of the latter are tall and narrow, while the Middle Magdalena urn bodies are usually relatively short and wide. Middle Magdalena urns often have a distinct neck separate from the shoulder while Lower Magdalena urns lack both shoulder and neck. The figure appears to be chanting. In South and Central American shamanism, it is held that shamanic power can be activated by means of "power songs." Power songs are used in healing rites to activate a shaman's power and alter the weather, among other things. Middle Magdalena River region. Middle Magdalena River regional style. Ca. A.D. 1100-1500. Grey-cream pottery. 27⅛" h. x 16⅜" w. Dallas Museum of Art; gift of Mr. and Mrs. Stanley Marcus (1985.166.A-B)

14.

16.

MÚCURA: SEATED FIGURE

In classic Muisca style the artist has used a
minimalist approach to define the human
figure. Arms and legs are indicated by fine fillets
of clay. Only the lower legs are indicated. The
placement of the hands on the knees implies
a seated posture. The serene expression of the
face depicts inner calm. The figure may
represent an idealized expression of rulership
or priesthood or a personage in Muisca myth or
cosmology. Muisca region. Muisca style.
Ca. A.D. 900-1600. Pottery with red and white
paint. 16½" h. x 10⅞" w. Instituto Colombiano
de Antropología (COLCULTURA) (MN-070).
Publications: Rojas de Perdomo 1995, p. 45.

17.

ANTHROPOMORPHIC VESSEL: SEATED FIGURE

This vessel shows clear artistic influence of
the classic Sinú cultures. The stem incorporates
a seated figure, the gender of which is not
indicated. The handle of the lid is in the form of
an animal with a long curled tail. The seated
posture with hands on knees is characteristic of the
widespread dignitary-seated-on-a-bench theme
although the bench is not visible in this example.
Provenance unknown. Malibú-related style.
Ca. A.D. 1300-1700. Mottled grey pottery.
10¼" h. x 8¾" w. Museo del Oro (CS4187).
Publications: Labbé, ed., 1992, no. S1.

FIGURE SEATED ON A BENCH

15.

The artist has used rectangular slabs of clay for the head and body of the figure and columns of clay for the
limbs. The result is a stylized human figure that imparts a sense of power and sublimity. The stylization of the
human form camouflages somewhat the fact that this is a depiction of the ubiquitous figure-seated-on-a-bench
theme. The bench has been abstracted by extending the slab body of the figure. The angulation of the legs
and thighs and the placement of the hands on the knees indicate a seated posture. The banded depressed
areas at upper arms, wrists, lower thighs, and ankles represent ligatures or bands intended to constrain the
flow of blood. It was believed that this strengthened the adjacent muscles. Middle Cauca region. Late
Quimbaya style. Ca. A.D. 1200-1400. Tan pottery. 13" h. x 10" w. Private collection

predominate in this style. In addition, historical sources confirm that women held considerable political power in this region, sometimes ruling entire provinces. There are isolated examples in substyles other than Betancí. Most are relatively small sculptures under eight or nine inches in height. A large example in a Malibú-related style found in the Lower San Jorge River region is the lid of a burial urn that incorporates a male figure seated on a bench (Bray 1978, no. 252).

Figures seated on a bench are common on decorated funerary urns found in a number of restricted styles characteristic of the Magdalena River region, which lies to the east of the Lower San Jorge River region. Its source is found far to the south in the region of San Agustín. Culturally and geographically, the river is divided into upper, middle, and lower reaches. In all styles, the theme, when portrayed, is on the lid of the urn.

In the Moskito style of the Lower Magdalena River region, the urns tend to be elongated and cylindrical with conical bases. The figures are relatively large, commonly with hands on knees (cat. no. 11), but a number of variants are known, including some in which the figure holds a lime flask or *poporo* (Labbé 1986, pl. 27).

Middle Magdalena urns are more ovoid and often have distinct necks and shoulders. They are often decorated with incised geometric patterns. Some examples portray more than one individual—sometimes even an entire family—seated on the same bench.

In an exceptional example from the Dallas Museum of Art (cat. no. 14) the figure's head is arched upward with mouth open as if singing. This work probably represents a shaman performing a power song, which was used in the neotropics to alter the weather, diagnose illness, or peer into the future. Power songs were sung to alter the shaman's consciousness and activate specific powers. In the Middle Magdalena region, freestanding renditions of the theme are also known (Bray 1978, no. 451).

The Tairona region, which lies along the Caribbean coast and adjacent lands of northern Colombia in the Department of Magdalena, is dominated by the Sierra Nevada de Santa Marta, an isolated mountain formation with peaks rising up to seventeen thousand feet above the nearby coast. A peculiarity of the Sierra is its diverse ecology, ranging from torrid desertlike environments to temperate and tropical forests. Snow-capped peaks overlook the Mediterranean-like climate of the Caribbean coast below.

The region was long an important center of development with certain threads of culture extending back in unbroken continuity for thousands of years. Even so, the theme appears relatively late in the prehistory of this region. At the time of the Spanish conquest, the region was dominated by the Tairona culture, one of Colombia's most sophisticated civilizations. The majority of examples can safely be dated to between 800 and 1600 A.D. and are fashioned in the Late Tairona style.

SEATED FEMALE FIGURE

The eyes are wide set and level with the nose, giving the face a foreshortened appearance. Much of the incising is shallow, with lines tightly spaced, imparting a shimmering effect to the design. The composition appears to be a Gulf of Urabá variant of the dignitary-seated-on-a-bench genre. The bench is suggested by the positioning of the legs and the placement of the hands on the upper thighs. Gulf of Urabá. Gulf of Urabá regional style. Date unknown. Cream-colored pottery. 6⅞" h. x 4¾" w. Museo del Oro (CS12791)

18.

Interestingly, most of the renditions in this style are restricted to ceramic forms such as *ocarinas* and small figural jars. Multitone flutelike musical instruments, *ocarinas* are hollow and often shaped in the form of a dignitary seated on a bench, with the ends of the bench usually in the form of dragon heads (cat. nos. 9, 13). In some examples, the bench is wing shaped (cat. no. 9). The central figure is often highly ornate, with elaborate dress, large earspools, a nose plaque, and lip plug. The head is usually crowned with a headdress. In many examples the tongue is distended and characterized by a median groove. To understand this iconography we may refer to the descendants of the Tairona, the Kogi Indians of the Sierra Nevada de Santa Marta.

In the belief system of the Kogi, the solar deity is described as sitting on a bench in the sky chewing coca, dispensing life in the form of sun rays. Elaborate dress and jewelry accentuate his high estate. The distended tongue in the Tairona compositions may allude to his beneficent self-sacrifice, as radiating sunlight is perceived as a sacrificial act in which the deity gives up his essence so that life on earth may exist. All life is engendered and sustained by the sun.

A groove along the length of the tongue implies duality, a concept central to native thought throughout the Americas. Among the Aztecs of Mexico, the distended tongue was associated with Tonatiuh, the solar deity, as a symbol of his autosacrifice. In Aztec myth, Nanahuatzin, the so-called "Diving God," sacrificed himself to become Tonatiuh (Labbé 1992, 121-23).

Small Tairona jars with a figure seated on a bench are almost identical to the *ocarinas* in iconography. The figure's hands on the *ocarina* are at or on the knees while figures on the jars usually hold a scepter or baton. Dragon heads often decorate the bench in both genres. Although the dragon may be modeled after a cayman, its meaning in the iconography of Colombia, Panama, and parts of Costa Rica appears to be related to the shamanic concept of *tinguna*, an emanation of power or energy from the "soul body" of a shaman or supernatural shamanic being. *Tingunas* are often portrayed in the prehispanic art of Central Panama as serpentine projections with cayman-like heads. The earliest depiction in Colombia of a dragon head used to represent a *tinguna* is found in a Late Ilama or Malagana-style goldwork (cat. no. 67). The dragon head has stylistic similarities to those

CANASTERO: SEATED FIGURE

19. The figure conveys a sense of pensive deliberation. The emphasis given to the shoulders is characteristic of the Malagana style. The band of triangular elements atop the head likely represents a crown, possibly of feathers. Department of Valle del Cauca. Malagana style. Ca. 150 B.C.-A.D. 200. Red-brown pottery. 4⅜" h. x 4⅜" w. Private collection

CANASTERO: SEATED OR SQUATTING FIGURE

20. The exaggerated bulbousness of the shoulders and upper arms conveys a tenseness in the posture that is reinforced by the open mouth and bared teeth. The positioning of the hands on the knees implies a seated posture, but the portrayal is unusual for seated figures, who are generally depicted as serene and calm. The intensity evoked suggests that the figure is in an altered state of consciousness. The vertical band of rectangular elements atop the head probably represents a diadem of feathers. Department of Valle del Cauca. Malagana style. Ca. 150 B.C.-A.D. 200. Pottery with red slip and white areas. 7¾" h. x 12" w. Private collection. Publications: Archila 1996, pl. 46.

seen in goldwork of Panama dating to between A.D. 400 and 700 and also to Tairona goldwork of later date. Among many groups in Colombia, the solar deity was considered First Shaman, the source of all subsidiary shamanic power (see Labbé 1995).

Among the Kalima, a coastal Venezuelan group, benches are decorated with a variety of animal forms—jaguar, turtle, and parrot—whose spirits are considered important animal auxiliaries of the shaman. The crocodile bench is associated with a great cayman personage said to govern aquatic creatures (Pineda Camacho 1994, 5; Zerries 1981, 350). The double-headed dragons on Tairona benches more directly represent emanations of shamanic power rather than a specific personage (although, as we shall see, the dual-natured cosmic cayman may be implied). In Tairona iconography the central figure seated on the bench is typically the key to identifying whether the figure is a shaman, ruler, or deity.

The cayman looms large in an important myth cycle shared by groups as widely dispersed as the Olmec of Mesoamerica and the Chavín Culture of northern Peru (Lathrap 1975, 56-57). Several elements of this cycle may help us understand the cayman imagery in certain Malamboid (cat. no. 159) and Late Tairona (cat. no. 13) artworks.

The myth conceives the entire universe as a giant cayman afloat in a boundless sea. This initial being gives birth to a cosmic dual-natured deity, a cayman of the sky, complemented by a subterranean aspect, a great cayman of the water and underworld. The cayman of the sky is closely associated iconographically with the harpy eagle while the cayman of the water and underworld is associated with large marine mollusks, particularly *Spondylus* and conchlike shells. This dual-natured deity is at one and the same time the phenomenal universe we experience and the source of all things within it (Lathrap 1975, 56-57). Communication among the sky cayman deity, humans, and the underworld cayman deity is expedited by the jaguar, the messenger and mediator between the sacred and secular worlds.

Since all phenomena result from the interaction and dynamic tension between these two complementary forces, it is in this sense that the two caymans are the source of all things and are conjoined. Their polar aspects, sky (male) and water-underworld (female), derive from an underlying oneness. The dynamic current engendered by their interaction is what is called fertility, and a prime role of the shaman is to act as the guardian of fertility.

Among Colombia's surviving native groups, a shaman's bench is distinguished from benches used by ordinary individuals. In certain cultures the distinctions may be based on decoration, size, or type of wood used. Among some groups plain benches are used by commoners while those decorated with animal motifs are associated with shamans. Among the Embera of the Choco

CANASTERO: SQUATTING FIGURE

The large, bulbous shoulders and the lack of detail in the rendering of the hands and feet are typical of the llama figural style. A seated figure with an arched crown or corona is a stock theme of the llama style of the Calima region. Cross-cultural study of the crown design on anthropomorphic figures suggests it may be an icon referencing the sun. Moreover, the sun is rendered anthropomorphically in both art and mythology among prehispanic and indigenous groups in Colombia. Calima region. llama style. Ca. 1000 B.C.-A.D. 1. Pottery with mottled brown slip. 11⅝" h. x 7¼" w. Museo del Oro (CC383)

21.

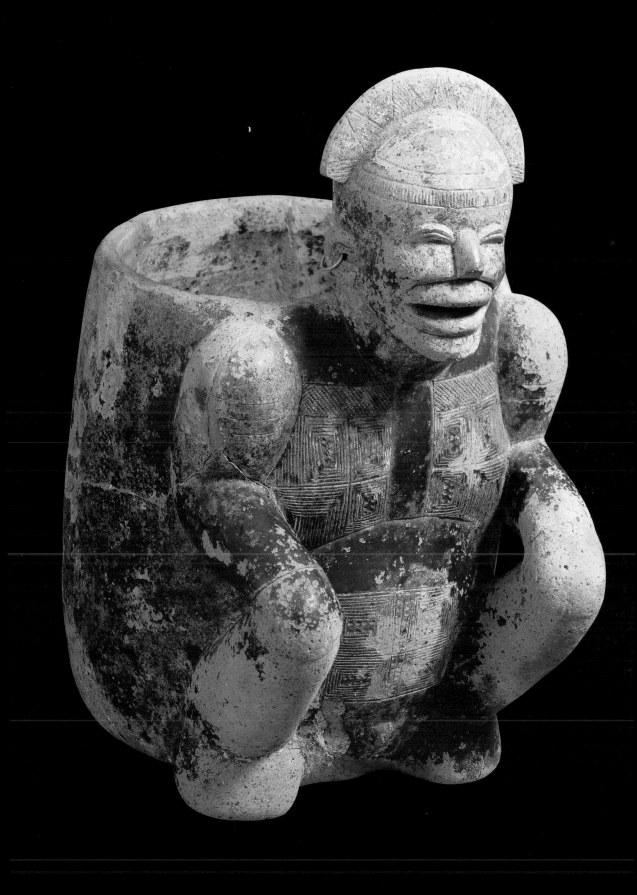

23.

PENDANT: SEATED DIGNITARY

The pendant comprises a bar supporting a seated figure. Danglers have been attached to the pendant by means of gold staples. The large headdress and bar held in the hands of the figure accentuate the high status and office of the central figure, who may represent either the solar deity or a priestly ruler. Muisca region. Muisca style. Ca. A.D. 900-1600. Gold. 3⅛" h. x 2⅞" w. Museo del Oro (7800). Publications: Labbé, ed., 1992, pl. M2, p. 61.

24.

FIGURAL JAR: RECLINING MALE FIGURE

The body of the figure is fused with the form of the "chair," with only a simple incised line separating the two. The figure's limbs emerge from the fused mass of body and chair. The reclining dignitary is a stock theme of unknown significance in Tairona art. His large labret and equally large nose plaque identify him as an elite member of his society. The avian pendant hanging from his neck suggests that he is a priest or possibly a deity like the solar culture hero found in Tairona mythology. Tairona region. Late Tairona style. Ca. A.D. 1000-1600. Black pottery. 8⅛" h. x 7⅞" w. x 9⅛" l. Private collection

FEATHERED HELMET

22.

The tall multicolored feathers (although modern replacements) accentuate the simple form and uniform gold of the cap. Feathered gold headgear was emblematic of the high status of the individual with whom it was buried. Middle Cauca region. Late Quimbaya style. A.D. 800-1600. Gold. 7⅛" h. x 3⅛" w. Museo del Oro (9319)

region, the material used determines whether a bench is intended for a shaman (Reichel-Dolmatoff 1960, 129; Pineda Camacho 1994).

The jaguar represents a variety of closely related concepts. In Colombia, it is clearly associated with shamanism and shamanic power. Among the Yucatec Maya, the *chilam* were upper-class priestly prophet teachers, in effect, shaman priests. A series of post-conquest manuscripts describing prehispanic myths and traditions of the Yucatec Maya were called Chilam Balam (from *chilam*, prophet; and *balam*, jaguar). It is noteworthy that all of the essential icons we observe in the myth—cayman, harpy eagle, and jaguar—are also preeminent iconography in the art of the Tairona.

A number of small jars (cat. no. 12) depict figures seated on undecorated benches. Often the figure's bulging cheek shows that he has a quid of coca in his mouth. No supporting iconography such as elaborate dress, regal posture, and cayman-headed bench defines him as the solar deity. Indeed, the figure is portrayed naked.

LIP ORNAMENT (LABRET)

The braid pattern on the two raised rectangular strips along the center of the labret is a common decorative element of Tairona goldwork. Labrets, or lip plugs, such as this are indicative of high status. Tairona region. Late Tairona style. Ca. A.D. 1000-1600. Gold. 1 ½" h. x ⅝" w. Museo del Oro (20778)

25.

A large sculpture in the collection of the Museo del Oro, Santafé de Bogotá, depicts a Tairona shaman-priest seated on a stool or bench (cat. no. 7). Dragon or serpent heads (iconographically the two are often interchangeable) are atop each side of the head. He grasps two serpent scepters, or perhaps emanations, i.e., *tingunas*.

Females seated on a bench or stool in Tairona art are extremely rare. They are usually rendered in a blackware substyle associated with groups who inhabited the coastal regions and adjacent low-lying foothills of the Sierra. A large example (cat. no. 6) portrays a seated naked female with hands on knees, a posture associated elsewhere with authority figures. In this instance, however, there is no supporting iconography such as scepter, jewelry, or other icons of chieftainship or elite status.

The Muisca region is an enchanted land embracing savannas and forests nestled in fertile highlands in the modern departments of Cundinamarca and Boyacá. The Muisca Indians and the closely related Guane had a long, continuous development in these lands. Late in their prehistory, in the centuries preceding the Spanish conquest, their power was consolidated into federations. Today, many of the inhabitants of Colombia's capital and largest metropolis, Santafé de Bogotá, as well as much of the rural population of the surrounding countryside, are descended from these indigenous peoples.

Realistic, freestanding figures seated on a bench are very rare in Muisca art, but a handful of examples in metal and ceramic are known. All are in styles that date to between A.D. 800 and 1540, the same period noted for this theme in the Tairona region.

The finest Muisca art is characterized by grace and elegance and a deliberate minimalist quality. There is also an inherent love of stylization, as exemplified in catalogue number 8, a figural jar in the form of an important personage seated on a bench. The artist has employed the jar as the body of the central figure. The neck of the jar, decorated with hatched, incised lines but devoid of any facial details, serves as the head. The arms and legs are formed of thin fillets of clay that contrast sharply with the full, ample body.

This imposing personage sits regally, dominating the scarcely adequate bench. For added support, the bench is shouldered by small Atlantean figures who strain beneath the central figure's enormous weight. The power and importance of the personage are further accentuated by large crisscrossed bands of stylized bird or animal pendants. Serpents meander across the abdomen. Diminutive human and animal figures are cradled in each arm, contrasting with the immensity of the central figure, who looms as a powerful supernatural personage.

The minimalist qualities of Muisca art are typified by the artistic characteristics of a large *múcura* (cat. no. 16), or spouted libation vessel. The spout of this vessel serves as the body of the central figure, but the bench is only implied by the positioning of the hands on the knees, suggesting a seated posture.

The Department of Nariño is characterized by three distinct geographic zones—the eastern tropical lowlands, the Andean highlands, and the Pacific coastal subregion. The highlands have a varied topography of rugged majestic peaks, pastoral valleys, and flat plains. The department's highland and Pacific coastal regions lie next to Ecuador, but the border did not exist prior to the imperial expansion of the Inca and the Spanish conquistadors. Consequently, many of the ancient archaeological cultures found on one side of the border are also found in adjacent regions on the other side.

FIGURE SEATED ON A BENCH
A male dignitary sits in regal posture on a double-headed crocodile bench. The back of the figure is modeled in the form of a small jar. Tairona region. Late Tairona style. Ca. A.D. 1000-1600. Black pottery. 4 ½" h. x 4 ½" w. Private collection

26.

The prehistory of Highland Nariño is not well documented for periods prior to A.D. 700. The main documented cultures in the region have been divided into three cultural complexes that correspond to the dominant art styles of the region: Piartal, ca. A.D. 750–1250; Capulí, ca. A.D. 850–1500; and Tuza, ca. A.D. 1250–1500.

Figures seated on a bench are common in the art of Highland Nariño. The most common theme is a dignified male figure seated on a bench with hands on knees typically painted in a black-on-red resist scheme. Female companion figures are depicted seated on the ground with legs and feet thrust forward. Variants include a figure with bowl or staff in hand. The renditions are realistic and lack the abstract qualities found in the Middle Cauca, Sinú, or Muisca regions.

In a second style, a cream-colored paint is used for the body of seated male figures while hair, bench, and breechclout may be painted either red or black. Negative resist decoration is not employed. Although these figures are usually postured with hands on knees, some are shown holding a child in the left arm. Most often the child looks back over the male figure's shoulder. In both styles there is some variation in the bench, although commonly it is a horizontal seat supported by two vertical planks. Actual benches were probably carved from a single block of wood.

Common to all styles is a bulge in the cheek of the male figure, usually on the left side. Because this feature seems to indicate the chewing of a wad of coca leaf, these figures are popularly referred to as *coqueros*.

As we have seen, the portrayal of a figure seated on a bench was a near-universal theme in the art of nearly all the major cultures within Colombia. Yet it is notably absent in the art of San Agustín and Tierradentro. Moreover, despite its wide distribution, the theme is often represented by only a few examples or in a single style in any one region. It is found in large numbers only in the Middle Cauca region, mostly in the form of *retablos*. In the Tairona region the theme is most often depicted in the form of *ocarinas* and very small figural jars, while in the Calima region, where it is distinctly rare, it may have been rendered in highly abstract form. Perhaps some of the *canastero* figures with hands on knees should be included, but the evidence is unclear.

The earliest depictions of the theme in unambiguous style appear to be the Tumaco examples (ca. 100 B.C.–A.D. 200), but we must allow for the possibility that it was earlier in the Calima region, given the somewhat ambiguous specimens in Ilama style noted earlier in the essay. What is clear is that the developmental thread begins in Southwest Colombia and proceeds northward and westward down the Cauca River valley, finding expression first in gold in Classic Quimbaya style (A.D. 0–800) and later (ca. A.D. 1000) in ceramics.

Dating the appearance of the theme in the Middle Sinú River region is problematic for certain substyles, but the examples in the Betancí style fall within the time parameters established for the Lower Magdalena, Tairona, Muisca, Middle Magdalena, and Highland Nariño regions—that is, sometime between A.D. 800 and 1540.

The overwhelming majority of figures seated on a bench are male. Where female companion pieces are present, they are seated on the ground with legs extended forward. Female companion pieces are most common in the Middle Cauca and in the Highland Nariño regions. The two exceptions—certain figures in Betancí style from the Sinú region, certain large blackware figures from the lower elevations of the Tairona region—sometimes feature females seated on a bench.

The most frequent variant portrays a dignified figure with head erect, looking forward and with hands placed on the knees. Such figures exude a sense of inner peace, contemplation, and authority. The next most common rendition is a figure holding a staff or

EAGLE PENDANT

The use of a gold-and-copper alloy is characteristic of Tairona goldwork. The typical braid pattern framing the head can also be seen at the neck and midsection. The stylized bird heads seen in profile at each side of the central bird's head and midsection suggest that this is not an ordinary bird but rather a depiction of a shaman who has undergone transformation, likely in "soul flight." Such pendants commonly hang from the necks of central figures in Tairona ceramic art. Tairona region. Late Tairona style. Ca. A.D. 1000-1600. Gold. 3⅜" h. x 2¾" w. Museo del Oro (13184). Publications: Bray 1978, fig. 299.

27.

scepter in one hand and perhaps a bowl in the other. This variant is probably associated with rulership, governance, and authority.

One of the many questions that remain to be answered is the identity of the personage portrayed. The solar deity as first Shaman is a good candidate in some cases—for example, the magnificent figure on a bench from Popayán, now in the collection of the Denver Art Museum (cat. no. 92). In other cases, however, the intent of the composition may be to focus attention on an ideal type, be it shaman, priest, ruler, or initiated member of the society. All are associated with benches in the ethnographic literature.

Another theme in Tairona art is a figure reclining in a chair rather than sitting on a bench (cat. no. 24). In objects in clay, jewelry indicates that this individual is of high status. Usually, the male genitalia are depicted, but we must be careful not to ascribe nudity to figures simply because genitalia are visible. Groups in the Amazon who use penis strings draw up the foreskin and tuck it under the string. Among such groups only an exposed glans, not any other part of the male anatomy, constitutes nudity.

One of this writer's colleagues was reminded of this concept while conducting ethnographic research among a Quechuan group residing in the tropical lowlands of Ecuador. A bush plane flew him to a clearing just outside the village. Alone and on foot he was suddenly besieged by village women, who proceeded to remove his clothing. All fell back in momentary shock, however, when they saw that he was circumcised. This discovery posed serious problems to local mores, for they assumed, since there was no foreskin in which to conceal the glans, that he was doomed to go about naked. Evidently, the women had learned that some American men are circumcised. Therefore, in order to protect their children from a display of outright nudity, they had rushed out to check the situation for themselves. They retreated to a hut, held a meeting, and devised a solution: they made a special penis string equipped with a small basketry cap to conceal the disturbing part of the anatomy.

It is often difficult to determine whether a penis string is implied. In a unique example found in Lake Guatavita in Muisca territory by Contractors Ltd. in 1911 (Bray 1978, no. 23), however, the figure is distinctly naked without a penis string. Moreover, the figure's arms

FUNERARY CHAIR

28. Ceramic funerary chairs appear to be restricted to the Middle Magdalena region. The figure of the shaman—unifier of sky and earth, of male and female forces—is incised on the front side of the back of the chair. Two serpents, representing the male and the female aspects of the life force, run along the perimeter of the chair. Middle Magdalena River region. Tolima style. A.D. 200-1600. Pottery with red-brown slip. 14½" h. x 7¾" w. x 11⅞" l. Museo del Oro (CTO849). Publications: For similar type see *Historia del Arte Colombiano* 1977, 384.

BENCH WITH OFFERING

29. The seat of the bench is bowed to suggest that it is stressing under its burden. The composition may represent an offertory jar placed on a bench. In actual usage the jar may have been a basket for gold offerings kept in a temple. The bench likely would have been wood. Provenance unknown. Malibú style. Ca. A.D. 1300-1700. Black pottery. 5" h. x 4⅜" w. Museo del Oro (CS4213). Publications: Pineda 1994.

NECKLACE PENDANT

30. Comprising ten zoomorphic figures apparently standing on a log, this pendant would have served as a centerpiece, either as part of a necklace or by itself, suspended around the neck. Gulf of Urabá. Gulf of Urabá regional style. Date unknown. Gold. ⅜" h. x 3⅜" w. Museo del Oro (MO-33080)

SEATED FEMALE FIGURE

SEATED DIGNITARY

are thrown back and support the head as if he is reclining in a carefree relaxed manner. But, appearances can be deceiving. The chair in this composition is somewhat similar to ceramic funerary chairs found in tombs in the Middle Magdalena region (cat. no. 28). The iconography on these small tomb chairs, which held a wrapped mummy, suggests shamanic associations. Similar chairs of appropriate size but made of perishable material may have been used by shamans. Shamanic chairs are more common in the goldwork of Colombia (fig. 2). Some are similar in form to those used by the Taino of the Caribbean (fig. 3).

It is possible that the Tairona compositions (cat. no. 24) and those from Lake Guatavita are also shamanic in nature. What appears to the modern eye as lounging may have been a position assumed for specific kinds of shamanic enterprise. Much work will be necessary among surviving indigenous groups throughout Latin America to document the variety of postures and positions assumed by shamans while performing rituals, a subject we will explore later in this essay. It is equally possible that the composition is purely allegorical, a theme derived from Tairona mythology. In some examples it is difficult to determine whether a metate or a bench is indicated. A metate could refer to the sun as the source of the life force found in food, because grain must be ground on metates for human consumption. In that case the carefree reclining posture would portray the personified solar deity as willingly giving his essence for mankind.

STANDING FIGURES

As noted earlier, the standing and seated postures held distinct meaning. Many of the standing female figures, for example, can be classified according to the positioning of the hands: (a) figures with hands placed on the hips (cat. nos. 46, 47, 48); (b) figures with hands at the breasts (cat. no. 52); or (c) figures with hands at the navel (cat. nos. 49, 50, 51, 55). Each of these categories draws attention to a specifically

SEATED FEMALE FIGURE (PRECEDING PAGES)

31.
The form is highly stylized: the ear ornaments meld with the arms, which fuse with the legs. The fusion of earspools and arms suggests animals, possibly felines seen in profile. The flanking of animal forms on each side of a central human figure is a convention used to represent shamanic personages assisted by their familiars. That animals are intended is indicated by the "pinched" earspools that form the ears of the animals. The body is elaborately decorated with rectilinear and curvilinear geometrics. The iconography suggests a female deity of great shamanic power. Caribbean Lowland region. Style and date unknown. Pottery. 9½" h. x 7½" w. Private collection. Publications: Labbé 1986, no. 99; Labbé 1988, no. 89.

SEATED DIGNITARY (PRECEDING PAGES)

32.
The earspools and scepter indicate elevated status. The necklace is composed of stylized bird elements. Identical necklaces in gold have been found. Muisca region. Muisca style. Ca. A.D. 900-1600. Pottery with red and white paint. 6½" h. x 5¼" w. Private collection

SEATED FEMALE DIGNITARY

33.
The mouth and eyes are formed identically and are given equal weight in the composition. The female genitalia is clearly indicated. The figure holds a bowl in one hand and a manikin staff in the other. Her elite status is indicated by the staff and items of dress. Muisca region. Muisca style. Ca. A.D. 900-1600. Pottery with red and white pigments. 10⅞" h. Museo del Oro (CM-12799)

female attribute: woman as procreator, woman as nurturer, or woman as protector of the young. While we would not consider the navel as a specifically female attribute, it is perceived as the point of contact between the child and the mother via the umbilicus.

Often there are stylistic conventions associated with a subtheme, irrespective of culture. Consider the following examples of standing female figures with hands on hips: catalogue numbers 46, 47, and 48. In all three figures great emphasis is placed on the large ample hips and full bulbous upper thighs. In addition, in numbers 46 and 48 there is a concave depression at the top of the head, possibly associating the personage portrayed with the moon deity.

An examination of another subtheme, figures representing standing females with hands at navel, reveals that the standard convention, regardless of region or substyle, is to place the hands at each side of the navel at the same level (cat. nos. 49, 50, 51). But a Middle Sinú River region work in Betancí modeled-and-incised style (cat. no. 55) is exceptional in placing the right hand above the navel and the left below. Of course, the validity of general

FUNERARY URN: SEATED FEMALE FIGURE (LEFT)

A naked female figure with hands resting on knees is seated atop the lid of a secondary burial urn. Typically, little attention has been placed on realism with respect to the fingers, which are distinguished by simple grooves and ridges. Secondary burial urns contained the gathered bones of the deceased. Bones were believed by some groups to be the seeds of new life and a vital link to the deceased. Lower Magdalena River region. Moskito style. Ca. A.D. 1000-1500. Pottery. 13⅜" h. x 9¼" w. Private collection

34.

SEATED MALE FIGURE (TOP RIGHT)

The nose, arms, and legs are rendered in typical Late Quimbaya style. The columnar structure of the torso and head deviates from the norm in that the torsos of Late Quimbaya figures tend to be considerably wider than they are thick. The torso in this specimen is more ovoid in configuration. Seated male figures in this style are almost invariably portrayed on a bench. It is unusual to find a male figure seated directly on the ground, which appears to have been a female prerogative. The bulbous calves result from the placement of ligatures above and below the calves, a practice carried on by some contemporary native groups in the Amazon basin such as the Mundé, who were only discovered just before World War I (see Levi-Strauss 1995, 174-85, for photo documentation of the practice by the Mundé). Archaeologically and stylistically this work is a companion piece to catalogue number 51. Middle Cauca region. Late Quimbaya style. Ca. A.D. 800-1600. Pottery. 9½" h. x 4½" w. Museo del Oro (CQ12801). Publications: Labbé, ed., 1992, pl. Q5.

35.

SEATED FEMALE FIGURE (CENTER RIGHT)

The semi-snarling mouth and the small holes placed at the corners of the mouth and eyes are reminiscent of 'artistic conventions used by preclassic cultures of Mexico, such as the Olmec. There are traces of resist decoration on the face. The short looped arms, which may have served as lugs, are in stark contrast to the large, bulbous legs. Emphasis is given to female anatomical attributes such as the vulva. The breasts and navel are connected by a painted triangle, with the apex of the triangle pointing to the genitalia. Added prominence is given to the vulva by the spread legs. Ironically, while the breasts are small and flat like those of a male, the feet have been converted into large oversized breasts. Baja Guajira region. Ranchería style. 500 B.C.-A.D. 1000. Pottery with red paint on white slip. 10⅜" h. x 9½" w. Museo del Oro (CR1574). Publications: Labbé, ed., 1992.

36.

ALCARRAZA: SEATED MALE FIGURE (LOWER RIGHT)

There is a sense of mass to the figure, which is accentuated by the large bulbous shoulders and upper arms and the equally large head. The oversized eyes and puckered mouth convey a dynamic power and intensity to the composition. The chamber of the *alcarraza* serves as the figure's body. The composition is a stock theme of undetermined significance in Ilama art. Calima region. Ilama style. Ca. 1000 B.C.-A.D. 1. Pottery with red-brown mottled slip. 8½" h. x 8½" l. Private collection

37.

artistic canons, principles, or conventions is not negated by such occasional deviations. It may be that a general law is intentionally modified to alter the intended symbolic message, that the artist is exercising artistic license, or in some cases that the artwork is a forgery.

Parent with child, a subtheme to be expected with female figures, is surprisingly rare in the prehistoric art of Colombia. The most common renditions are found in clay in the Capulí style of Highland Nariño, most often in the form of a male figure seated on a bench with the child in his left arm. Examples of female figures with child in this style have also been found, but the infant is cradled horizontally in the mother's arms. It is surprising, given the vital importance of the mother-child relationship in the indigenous cultures of Colombia, that the theme was not more widespread in art.

An elegant example from the Middle Sinú River region in Betancí modeled-and-incised style (cat. no. 44) consists of a standing female bearing a large jar atop her head and cradling a smaller figure in her left arm. The smaller figure's features appear somewhat mature, certainly not infantlike. Although we cannot be certain, it is possible the central figure represents a deity or goddess, rather than a human mother, and the small figure a human adult entrusted to the deity for initiation. Naturally, without substantiation, such an interpretation is nothing more than mere conjecture and hypothesis, but so is the alternative view that a natural mother and infant are represented.

In a rare *canastero* example of the mother-and-child theme in the Ilama style of the Calima region, the mother is a towering, powerful standing figure (cat. no. 45). The comparatively frail and diminutive child suckles at her breast. The artist has imparted massive volume to every part of the mother's body. Her huge oversized feet are equal to the task of holding up her massive legs and torso. Her large muscular arms easily support the weight and form of the infant. The mother looks forward with joy and assurance. Indeed, the work has sculptural qualities reminiscent of the internationally recognized Colombian artist Botero.

Figures with child from the Middle Cauca region are also uncommon and are usually rendered with the adult in seated posture, a trait shared with depictions of the theme in the Highland Nariño region. An unusual example in the *retablo* style depicts a female figure with child seated on the ground (cat. no. 40). The child is individually sculpted but placed within the contours of the female's embracing arms. The simplicity of line in depicting

KNEELING FEMALE DIGNITARY

38.

This work is among the largest figures in this style. Most range from three to five inches high. The flat top of the head is characteristic of this style. The large nose ornament, necklace, and pectoral identify her as a female deity or an elite member of her society. Middle San Jorge River region. Montelibano style. Ca. A.D. 800-1000. Buff pottery. 9⅜" h. x 6" w. Museo del Oro (CS5932)

39.

40.

SEATED MALE FIGURE WITH CHILD

SEATED FEMALE FIGURE WITH CHILD

The figure is rendered in the *retablo* style. The term *retablo* connotes a flat board in Spanish. Both male and female figures in this style are sometimes depicted holding a child. Males are invariably shown seated on a bench, which is formed by extending the slab from the buttocks to the ground. The tubular legs are slightly bent at the center to suggest the seated posture. This composition may portray a father in idealized form, a deity such as the Sun Father accepting or receiving a young initiate, or perhaps the deceased, as these sculptures are usually found in graves. Middle Cauca region. Late Quimbaya style. Ca. A.D. 1200-1400. Tan pottery with traces of resist decoration. 10⅛" h. x 7" w. Private collection

The genre is that of the *retablo*. Painted designs on *retablos* are usually rendered by means of the resist technique. Here the child or young initiate is an individual sculpture. The personage appears to be highly composed and severe. The artistic intent may be to portray an ideal mother or motherhood. An alternative explanation is that the Earth Mother is accepting a newly initiated member of the community or possibly the deceased, as the sculpture was likely found in a grave. Middle Cauca region. Late Quimbaya style. Ca. A.D. 1200-1400. Tan pottery. 10¼" h. x 7¾" w. Private collection. Publications: Labbé 1986, pl. 19; Labbé 1988, pl. 19.

ALCARRAZA: KNEELING FEMALE FIGURE

This composition represents a common theme in the Ilama-style art of the Calima region. The figure is kneeling with eyes closed as if in deep contemplation. A braided necklace with pendant hangs from the neck. Rosettes either delineate nipples or indicate breast ornaments. Calima region. Ilama style. Ca. 1000 B.C.-A.D. 1. Pottery with red-brown slip. 12⅞" h. x 6" w. Private collection

ALCARRAZA: KNEELING FIGURE

The hemispherical incised eyes and use of white to highlight areas are characteristic of the Malagana style. A naked female figure in a half kneeling position adjusts her loaded burden bag, which is carried tumpline fashion, suspended from her head. The significance of this composition may be allegorical in nature. Department of Valle del Cauca. Malagana style. Ca. 150 B.C.-A.D. 200. Pottery with red slip and added white. 11⅜" h. x 7½" w. Private collection. Publications: Rojas de Perdomo 1995, cover; Archila 1996, pl. 48-48a.

NECKLACE (FOLLOWING PAGES)

The necklace is composed of variably sized beads made up of clusters of small globular elements. Calima region. Yotoco style. A.D. 1-800. Gold. ⅛" l. median average of each bead. Museo del Oro (5367)

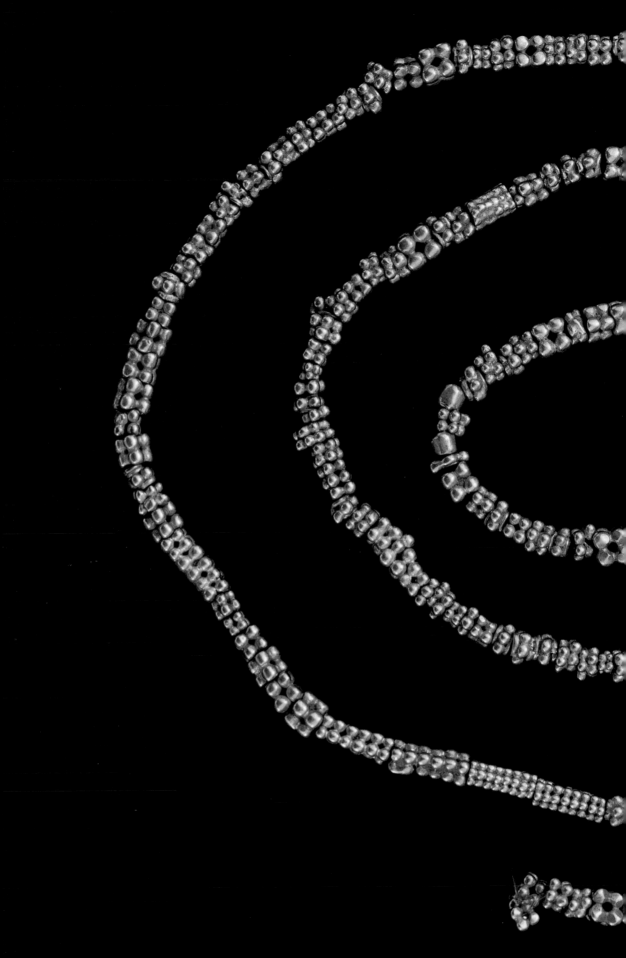

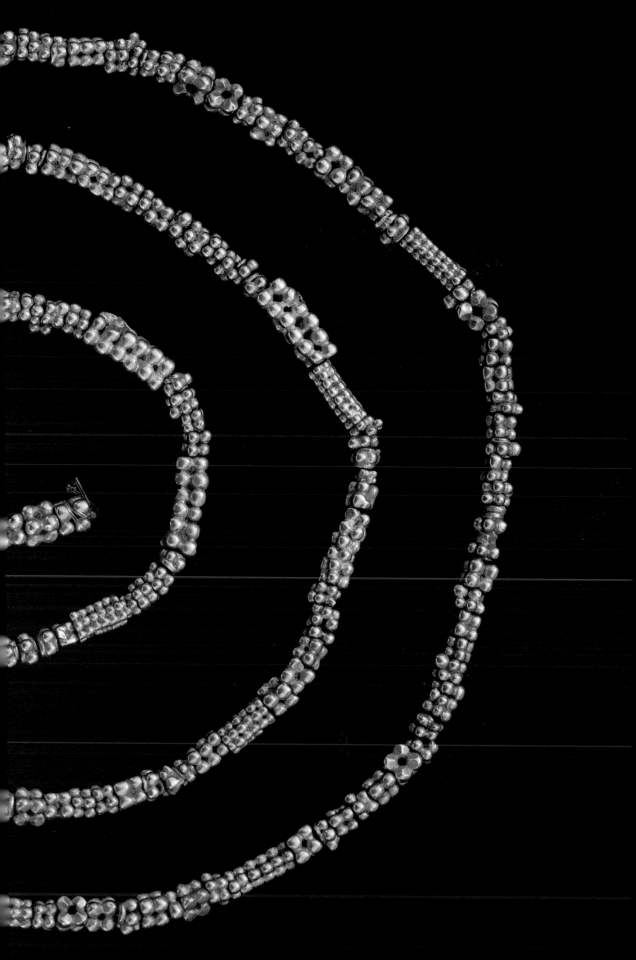

eyes and mouth imparts a sense of stolid dignity to the composition. The passive assurance of the mother contrasts with the expressive resignation of the child figure, whose foreshortened arms and hands are spread wide in seeming anticipation. The contour of the child's body and the back-angled head accentuate its helpless, dependent condition.

In a second example in the *retablo* style (cat. no. 39), the central figure is seated on a bench, implied by the extension of the slab below the juncture of the legs to the body, the 90-degree angling of the legs at the knee, and the placement of the right hand on the leg. Although the gender is not indicated, a male figure seems to be implied by the seated posture and bench. The child is cradled in the figure's left arm, facing the adult figure. It is noteworthy that in male figures with child in Colombian art, the child either faces the adult or peers backward over his shoulder.

fig. **3**

RECLINING STOOL
Dominican Republic. Taino culture.
Wood with gold inlay.
Musée de l'Homme, Paris.
Drawing by Joseph Kramer.

SHAMANS AND PRIESTS

Shamanism is probably coeval with the appearance of man in the New World. Powerful shamanic traditions still thrive in many parts of the Americas today, particularly in the tropical forest cultures of Central and South America. Over much of Colombia, shamans traditionally existed side by side with institutionalized priestcraft. In some cases, however, it is perhaps more instructive to speak of shaman-priests than to view them separately, for the practitioner often combines attributes of both roles.

It is especially difficult to distinguish the two in the Colombian context. A shaman's knowledge is empirical, gained firsthand through direct experience. Often his or her training entails the ingestion of plants or other substances that can induce altered states of consciousness or excite mental faculties dormant in normal states of being. The use of psychomimetic substances in traditional indigenous contexts was ritually controlled and supervised by an experienced practitioner. The novice shaman also undergoes in-depth instruction in natural history, herbalism, and indigenous perceptions of natural law.

MOTHER AND CHILD

44.

The profuse use of incising for details is typical of this style. Figures rendered in this style impart a sense of deep calm and inner resolve. As in this large example, the eyes are generally coffee-bean shaped. Although this motif is commonly interpreted as representing a mother and child, alternative interpretations are possible. The figure may represent a goddess or other supernatural personage. The "child's" features and elaborate hairstyling are suspiciously mature looking. Middle Sinú River region. Betancí modeled-and-incised style. Ca. A.D. 1000-1500. Light brown pottery. 13 ¼" h. x 6 ⅜" w. x 7 ¼" l. Fondo de Promoción de la Cultura (S-12566). Publications: Bray 1978, no. 246; *Arte de la Tierra, Colombia: Poder* 1994, no. 29; *Arte de la Tierra, Colombia: Sinú y Río Magdalena* 1992, no. 15.

The shaman functions as healer, counselor, social mediator, and oftentimes leader of his or her group.

What distinguishes the shaman from an ordinary healer, religious counselor, secular leader, or knowledgeable individual, however, are distinct shamanic powers. Shamans are believed able to travel out of body in their "spirit forms," a phenomenon referred to as "soul flight." In addition, an especially powerful shaman is believed capable of altering the shape of his spirit form at will and assuming the form and characteristics of other species, such as birds or jaguars. It is not the physical body, however, that is transformed but the "spirit body."

Shamans are said to communicate with animals and enlist them as spirit allies or physical auxiliaries. In certain traditions shamans use chants or power songs to awaken and activate shamanic powers, which include the ability to look into a person's body to diagnose the nature and cause of an illness or disease, the ability to see distant events far from the shaman's physical self, or even the power to alter natural law and change the weather.

By contrast, the knowledge of priests is acquired through oral tradition, not necessarily tested or proved by direct experience. They are also likely to be specialists in ritual who perform only at specific rites and ceremonies. The priest's role is generally more socially and ceremonially defined than the shaman's. To the extent that a priest is also capable of exercising shamanic powers he is a shaman-priest rather than mere religious ritualist.

Certain shamanic themes recur in the prehispanic art of South and Central America. The most common depict empowered shamans, shamans undergoing spirit body transformation, and shamans in flight or soul travel.

Empowered shamans are usually distinguished by such artistic conventions as *tingunas* extending from the shaman's body. In gold art they often take the form of serpentine projections from the shaman's body with the head of a crocodilian or dragon (cat. no. 67; Labbé 1995). In the indigenous mind, vital energy is the essence of life. It empowers the shaman to promote the fertility of plant, animal, and human.

As the mediator and guardian of fertility, the shaman harmonizes the many dual-natured complementary forces that support the natural world. The shaman mediates sky and earth, male and female, and myriad benevolent and malevolent manifestations in the everyday life of the community.

The shaman's role as mediator is often rendered in schematized form in goldwork (cat. no. 68). In ceramic art, paired complementary geometrics often decorate the shaman's torso (cat. nos. 84, 96), a convention also widely used in the prehispanic art of Central Panama. Paired triangles, sometimes arranged in butterfly patterns, are commonly associated with concepts of fertility and transformation.

A Tolima goldwork (cat. no. 68) illustrates the point. Here, the shaman's role as unifier of sky and earth (male and female powers, respectively) is symbolized by paired

CANASTERO: MOTHER NURSING CHILD

Canasteros, figures with cylindrical jars attached to their back, are common in Ilama ceramic art. Here, the body structure of the mother is massive. The suckling child is secure in her mother's strong arms. Calima region. Ilama style. Ca. 1000 B.C.-A.D. 1. Pottery with red-brown slip. 9⅛" h. x 9⅜" w. Museo del Oro (CC4476)

45.

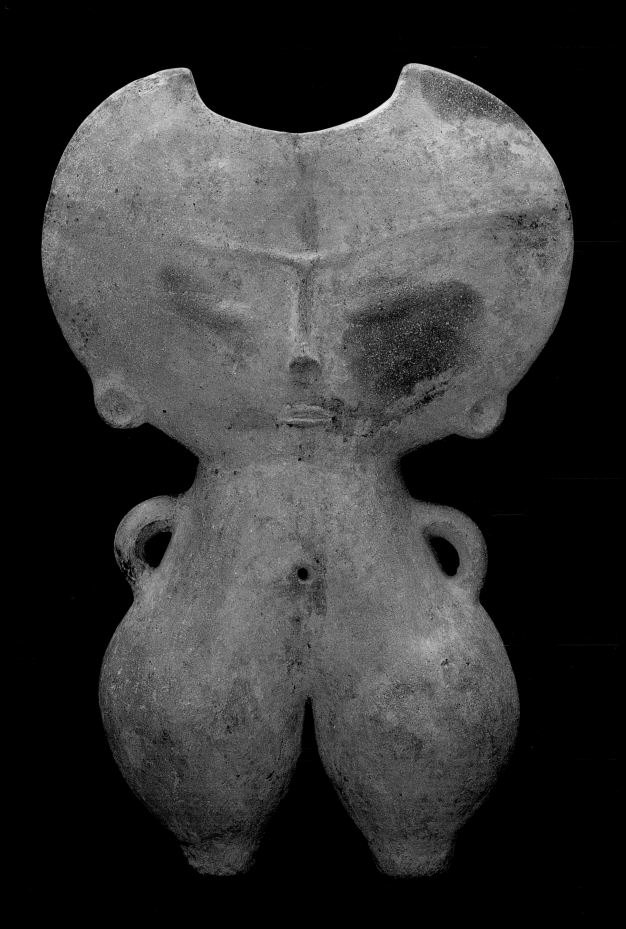

47.

STANDING FEMALE FIGURE

The figure has coffee-bean shaped eyes,
a foreshortened face, and voluminous thighs.
The iconographic emphasis on womanly
attributes—pronounced breasts, well-delineated
navel, and ample hips—directs attention
to her procreative potential. Northern Colombia.
Style and date unknown. Black pottery.
15⅜" h. x 9" w. Private collection.

48.

STANDING FEMALE FIGURE

The neck is barely indicated, the foreshortened
arms are more lugs than limbs, and the hips and
upper legs are disproportionately massive. The
head and face of this figure are distinctively feline
in appearance and may represent a transformed
shamanesss in jaguar guise. Lower Magdalena
River region. Style unknown. Ca. A.D. 1300-1700.
Black pottery. 9⅛" h. x 3⅜" w.
Bowers Museum of Cultural Art (96.70.1)

STANDING FEMALE FIGURE

46.

The only other sculpture in this style and form in a public collection is in the collection of the Museo del Oro,
Santafé de Bogotá. The arms of this figure are little more than lugs. The head has the appearance of a
crescent moon. The phallic configuration of the torso and legs and the manner in which it is articulated with
the head of the figure suggest fertility. Caribbean Lowland region. Caribbean Lowland regional style.
Date unknown. Pottery with red-brown slip. 10⅜" h. x 7" w. Private collection. Publications: Labbé 1986,
no. 93; Labbé 1988, cover and no. 93.

71.

stepped frets used as arms and legs. The hands are raised upward to the sky, the feet complementarily positioned downward toward the earth. The tail-like extension with two in-curving projections are schematized *tingunas*. The curvilinear form represents female powers. In neotropical shamanism, female linear expressions are curvilinear and male expressions rectilinear. Female forces move downward toward the earth and subterranean space while male forces move upward, linking with the powers of the sky (see Labbé 1995 for an analysis of native gender-based classification systems). The projections above the figure's head are rectilinear and therefore male. They are positioned to oppose one another, in direct contrast to the posterior tail-like curvilinear projections.

Shamans in soul flight are rendered either as birds with certain human elements or as human figures with avian characteristics. An excellent example is a goldwork in Tolima style (cat. no. 69) that retains the shamanic male-female *tingunas* observed in catalogue number 68 but in more abstract style. In number 69, bifurcation is intentionally blurred to serve as the shaman-bird's tail. Still, the head in number 69 is clearly more humanlike than avian.

In neotropical shamanism practitioners assume a variety of postures to activate their powers in preparation for shamanic undertakings. Many of these postures have been recorded on film, but more by chance than deliberate study. We will not understand the true significance of these various body postures within the context of shamanism without concerted, systematic ethnographic research.

Clearly, posture is significant in the art of prehispanic Colombia. Numerous postures recur, such as seated position, with legs crossed (cat. no. 86), squatting positions (cat. nos. 80, 84), and kneeling positions (cat. no. 82). Some postures appear to be unique, like a Malagana figure with the right leg placed across the left thigh and the left hand placed against the sole of the right foot (cat. no. 81). Others are uncommon, like an Ilama seated figure with the soles of both feet positioned inward fronting one another (cat. no. 79).

As noted above, the ethnographic literature is all but silent on the subject of shamanic posture. An exception is a Muisca goldwork, a seated personage with arms hugging knees (cat. no. 83). According to Tukano shamans, this posture is used to enhance concentration and heighten perception. A shaman in this position often stares intensely at a flame (Reichel-Dolmatoff 1988, 44). Presumably, this stance induces a trance that initiates an altered state of consciousness and activates shamanic power.

More specifically, this posture, frequently seen in Muisca goldwork, is a seated position in which the arms embrace the knees. The knees push against the arms as they pull the knees inward, thereby creating dynamic tension between the two forces. The knees are not

FEMALE FIGURAL PEDESTAL BOWL

49.

Incising is typical of the Betancí style. Here the artist has skillfully modeled the stem of the cup or bowl as a female dignitary, likely a deity. The skirt is decorated with rhomboid patterns, a preeminent geometric form used by Betancí ceramists. Although we do not know what significance this had for the Sinú, among other groups, such as the Tukano, the rhomboid is a symbol of female genitalia and women's procreative power. Middle Sinú River region. Betancí modeled-and-incised style. Ca. A.D. 1000-1500. Light brown pottery. 11⅞" h. Museo del Oro (CS12857)

50.

STANDING FEMALE FIGURE

The bulbous shoulders and thighs in combination with a narrow waist are typical of this style, as is the profuse body decoration indicated by incised lines and geometrics. The figure's hands are placed on the abdomen aside the navel. This and the large well-defined vulva are likely an allusion to her procreative function. Gulf of Urabá. Gulf of Urabá regional style. Date unknown. Cream-colored pottery. 7 ½" h. x 4 ⅛" w. Museo del Oro (CS12792)

51.

STANDING FEMALE FIGURE

The narrow groove used to separate the head from the body is typical of this style. The eyes, although of a modified coffee-bean type, are not as puffed as in other styles. The hands, placed aside the abdomen, focus attention on the procreative power of the female form. This work is a companion piece to catalogue number 35. Middle Cauca region. Late Quimbaya style. Ca. A.D. 800-1600. Pottery with weathered surface. 9⅜" h. x 7 ½" w. Museo del Oro (CQ12802)

STANDING FEMALE FIGURE

The trapezoidal head, coffee-bean shaped eyes, and soft rounded contours of the body are typical traits of the Late Quimbaya style. Late Quimbaya artists preferred abstract cubist human forms over the stylistic realism favored by the earlier Classic Quimbaya style. The schematized arms placed in relief upon the broad chest accentuate the fullness and inherent power of the female form. Middle Cauca region. Late Quimbaya style. Ca. A.D. 800-1600. Pottery with white and black on red slip. 14" h. x 9⅜" w. Museo del Oro (CQ 540)

52.

54·

JAR WITH PAIRED FIGURES IN RELIEF

This jar features a recurrent but rare theme in Betancí art. Females played important roles in the cultures of the Sinú and predominate in the art as well. In a composition repeated on each side of the vessel, a pair of female dignitaries hold hands. The vessel's geometric decoration reflects the dualism inherent in the main motif. The triangles are arranged in pairs, and sets of black triangles are contrasted with light-colored triangles. Middle Sinú River region. Betancí modeled-and-incised style. A.D. 1000-1500. Pottery with black on light brown slip. 13½" h. x 15" d. Private collection. Publications: Labbé 1986, pl. 26; Labbé 1988, pl. 26.

55·

STANDING FEMALE DIGNITARY

The figure is unusually large and the placement of the left hand is also uncommon. In most examples, both hands are placed aside the navel and at the same level. Representing an individual of elite status, possibly a goddess, the figure is wearing a wraparound skirt decorated with panels containing crossed-bar design elements. The incised design on the figure's chest and abdomen is bilateral and consists of bands of chevrons. Middle Sinú River region. Betancí modeled-and-incised style. Ca. A.D. 1000-1500. Light brown pottery. 13¼" h. x 6" w. Private collection

STANDING MALE FIGURE

53·

Large figural sculpture in clay is rare in pre-Columbian art from Colombia and is usually in the Tumaco style. The posture here suggests a ritual pose. The wide open mouth may indicate chanting. The geometric stepped frets on the figure's kilt are widespread designs in the Americas. Among those groups that still assign meaning to these geometrics, they are said to represent interacting clouds with lightning as negative design formed by the space between the clouds. The composition likely represents a shaman or priest petitioning the sky for rain. The holes along the edge of the ears may have served to hold gold ornaments such as rings or studs. Pacific Coastal region, Department of Nariño. Tumaco-La Tolita style. 300 B.C.-A.D. 300. Pottery with red paint. 26⅞" h. x 14⅜" w. x 5½" l. Fondo de Promoción de la Cultura (T-12384). Publications: Bray 1978, no. 513; *Arte de la Tierra, Colombia: Tumaco* 1994, p. 45; *Arte de la Tierra, Colombia: Poder* 1994, no. 17.

allowed to come up against the chest. Often, the shaman's mouth is open, possibly indicating the chanting or singing of a power song. Power songs are integral to many shamanic rituals. Ritual necessitates an officiate, material paraphernalia, sacred space, and a desired result. As cultural power used to mediate the forces of nature, ritual is the means whereby various dimensions of being, including the psychological realms, are brought into functional relationship.

Reality in the native perception is a multidimensional yet intrinsically holistic realm. In other words, every part is in some way related to every other part. Indigenous ecology not only includes species visible to the senses, it also affirms the existence of numerous beings and sentient entities invisible to normal perception. The multidimensional realms can be accessed, manipulated, and explored. Ritual accesses power from one or more of these realms to the benefit of the human community.

In Colombia, the majority of figures with open mouths are found in the Department of Nariño and are rendered in the Capulí style (A.D. 850–1500), but some are also found in the art of Calima and the Middle Magdalena (cat. no. 14). The portrayals may be either human or animal forms. Often the head is angled upwards, perhaps to show that the song is directed skywards as a petition for rain. In the ceramic art of Nariño, many of these figures are in the form of a frog. Groups in the Amazon believe that the croaking of frogs promotes rainfall; in other words, the frog's croaking is viewed as a form of power song.

In a rare example of a burial urn from the Middle Magdalena River region (cat. no. 14), the figure sits on a bench. Although figures seated on benches are not unusual in the funerary art of the Middle Magdalena, few are portrayed chanting.

An example from the Cauca region in Malagana style incorporates a standing zoomorph performing a ritual (cat. no. 89). It is difficult to determine which species of animal is intended.

In another example in this style (cat. no. 93), the shaman-singer has an animal familiar or alter-ego attached to his back. Animal familiars or alter-egos are rare in the clay art of Colombia. When portrayed they most often come from the Tumaco and Calima regions. They are not uncommon, however, in the monumental stone sculpture of the San Agustín region.

ANTHROPOMORPHIC VESSELS

The most common prehispanic figural art in Colombia are ceramic anthropomorphized or humanlike jars, bowls, bottles, and other similar forms. The vessels were personified by adding human characteristics to the basic vessel form, by means of appliqués, incising, painting, or modeling.

STANDING FIGURE

The feline atop the head suggests that the personage is either a priest or a shaman. Pacific Coastal region, Department of Nariño. Tumaco-La Tolita style. Ca. 300 B.C.-A.D. 300. Grey-white pottery. 19¾" h. x 9½" w. Museo del Oro (CT12819)

56.

58.

PENDANT: ANTHROPOMORPHIC FIGURE

The figure has a crown or corona around its head and holds an object in each hand. Department of Valle del Cauca. Late Ilama or Malagana style. Ca. 200 B.C.-A.D. 200. Gold. 1 ⅜" h. Private collection

STANDING PAIRED FIGURES

57. The Malagana style typically employs more incised decoration than the contemporary Yotoco style of the Calima region. Here two figures are joined back to back. The distended stomach may be an allusion to the procreative power of the female or may indicate pregnancy. Department of Valle del Cauca. Malagana style. Ca. 150 B.C.-A.D. 200. Pottery with red and white slip. 7 ⅛" h. x 4 ¾" w. Private collection. Publications: Archila 1996, pl. 54.

59.

PRIEST OR RULER WITH BOWL

A priest or ruler appears to be holding three rattles in each hand. The bowl resting on the knees suggests either an offering or a receptacle waiting to be filled. Department of Magdalena. Chimila-related style. Date unknown. Buff pottery. 6 ½" h. x 4 ½" w. Private collection

60.

STANDING MALE VOTIVE FIGURE (TUNJO)

This human figure is rendered in a schematic fashion typical of the Muisca style. The arms and legs are fashioned of extremely thin fillets of metal. Depicted with an erect phallus, the figure holds a staff in one hand and an unidentified implement consisting of two thin rods in the other. A coiled ornament hangs from each arm. Figures such as this were placed in votive jars, sometimes with raw uncut emeralds. Muisca region. Muisca style. Ca. A.D. 900-1600. Gold. 9" h. x 1 ⅜" w. Museo del Oro (32868)

The extent of vessel modification is highly variable. In some cases, the anthropomorphized vessel is given a face and limbs (cat. no. 98); in others, little more than a face distinguishes the form (cat. no. 97). In other examples, the entire human form is portrayed, the jar serving as the figure's body (cat. no. 101).

Works such as catalogue number 100 are so stylized and abstract that only a trained eye can discern the intended face. In this example, the face is modeled around the neck of the jar. The eyes are tiny appliqués positioned far apart, and a short flange serves to divide the face from the neck. The most realistic human attribute is the nose, but even this feature is disproportionately small. A labret is visible along the flange. The composition is skillfully executed, and the overall effect is balanced and elegant.

Catalogue number 107, an anthropomorphic burial urn exemplifies the use of appliqué to render human characteristics—in this case, arms, legs, and facial traits. The rounded contours of the shoulder of the jar are complemented by the contours of the lid, which also serves as the figure's head. The arms, decorated with numerous bangles, are formed by thin ropelike fillets of clay placed in relief along the shoulder of the vessel. The abbreviated thighs emerge from the vessel's surface and are dwarfed by the disproportionately large bulbous calves enveloped by numerous anklets.

Catalogue number 103, an anthropomorphized jar rendered in the Late Quimbaya style, appears to be allegorical. The artist has contrasted the oversized limbs and exaggerated female genitalia of the lower body with the undersized head and slender foreshortened arms of the upper body. Perhaps this distortion is intended to caricature the effects of over-indulgence in

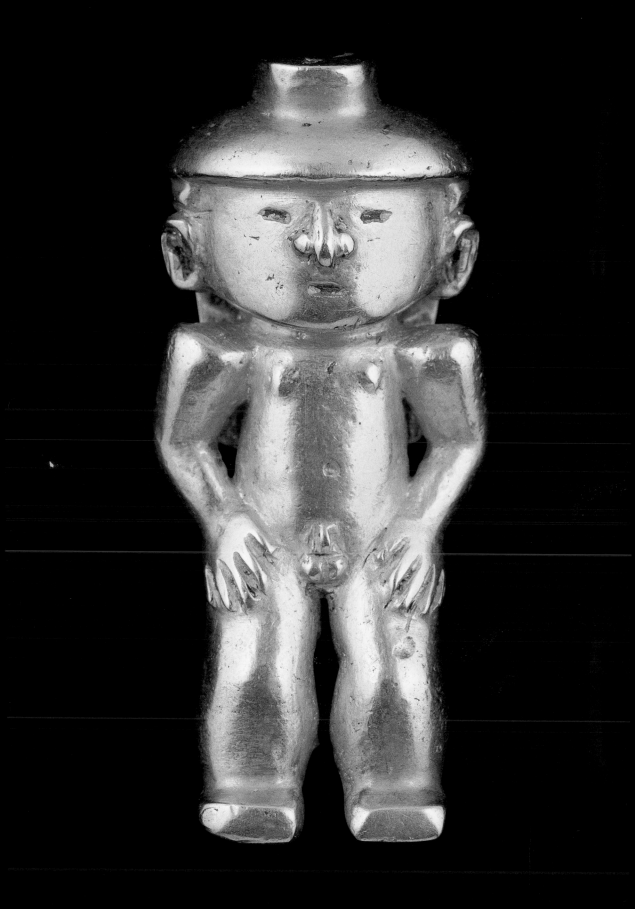

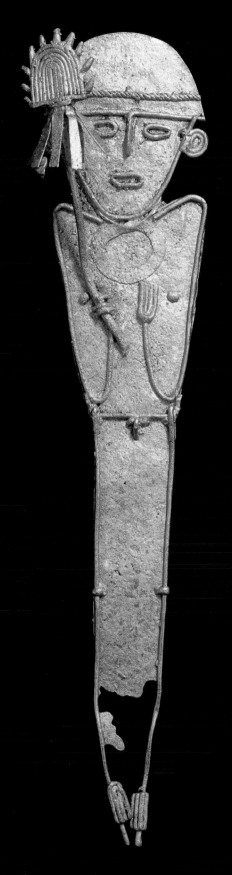

STANDING MALE VOTIVE FIGURE (TUNJO)

65238

FIGURAL JAR: STANDING FEMALE

sex or to portray an individual whose life is somehow out of balance. Whatever the original intent, the power of this artwork transcends the boundaries of time and culture.

A Quimbaya-style anthropomorphic bowl has arms and legs rendered in relief with modeled head and feet (cat. no. 109). The figure appears to be holding herself open in acceptance of her role as receptacle.

Some anthropomorphic vessel forms are characteristic of specific areas. *Alcarrazas* and *canastero* forms, for example, are typical of the Calima region. The *múcura* was characteristic of the Muisca and Guane Indians of the Eastern Cordillera. The so-called chieftain jars, on the other hand, are associated with the Tairona of the Sierra Nevada de Santa Marta.

The *alcarraza* is a double-spouted vessel characterized by an enclosed chamber and two tapering spouts. A band of clay connects the spouts and serves as a handle (cat. no. 37). The form is, strictly speaking, more or less a bottle, although it is unlikely that it actually functioned as such. Rather, it was commonly used as a vehicle of artistic expression to communicate themes relevant to indigenous culture.

In anthropomorphized variants, modeling, incising, pinch-molding, and painting are used to create details of head, face, or limbs, as well as items of dress and body decoration. The vessel chamber serves as the figure's body, which may be realistic (cat. no. 42), abstract, or highly stylized (cat. no. 37). Appliqué is not used as a decorative technique on this vessel form.

The *canastero* form is essentially a cylindrical open-mouthed figural jar. The front of the jar is modeled in either human or animal shape (cat. no. 21). Since the back of the vessel remains unmodified, it appears as if the figure is carrying a jar or basket on its back. This variant of *canastero* is specific to the Calima region and is most often rendered in the Ilama style, although some in Malagana style are known (cat. no. 20). The form is also found in the Tumaco-La Tolita culture. Many of the anthropomorphic *canasteros* are characterized by a crown or corona at the head, usually in the form of vertical elements arranged in a curving band (cat. no. 20), possibly representing feathers or rays. Another common crown takes the form of a curved band of triangles or rows of interlocking triangular bands (cat. no. 21), possibly indicating a Calima version of the solar deity.

Specifically associated with the Muisca and Guane Indians of the Eastern Cordillera, the *múcura* is characterized by a globular chamber and a tall cylindrical spout with handle. The anthropomorphizing of the vessel is always restricted to the spout. In some cases little more than the face of the intended figure is portrayed (cat. no. 104). Details of the face may be painted, pinch-molded, or appliquéd. In other examples, appliquéd arms and legs are used to give the figure a more full-bodied appearance.

The images used to decorate the spouts of these vessels are probably portrayals of personages such as the goddess Bachue or the Muisca culture hero Bochica-Nemquetheba. Bachue, the mother of mankind, was the patroness of springs, lakes, lagoons, and agriculture. Soon after the creation of light by the creator Chiminigagua she emerged from the depths of a sacred lake, identified in Muisca legend as Lake Iquaque, bearing an infant son. Once he matured, she coupled with him to bring forth mankind. Thereafter, she and her son assumed the form of serpents and returned to the watery depths.

There is considerable religious symbolism in this myth. In the esoteric lore of many native groups, life results from the union of the female and male aspects of the life force, said to manifest itself in the real world by permeating the medium of water, resulting in protoplasm, blood, and chlorophyll. In pre-Columbian iconography, the serpent is the symbol par excellence of the life force.

A number of Muisca painted bowls are decorated with two complementary serpents. Whether rendered in painted form or attached to the sides of the bowl as appliqués, these serpents most likely represent the sacred couple Bachue and her son. Since the *múcura* was used to store or dispense liquids, the spout can be viewed as emerging from the body of the vessel much as Bachue emerged from the lake.

The fuller-bodied representations—that is, those in which the modification of the spout also includes arms and legs—typically appear to depict a male personage (cat. no. 16). The face is framed by thin fillets of clay, and objects denoting rank and status, such as staffs, are often held in the hands. The identity of the personage depicted is difficult to determine. He may represent the son of Bachue, but there are no specific iconographic elements to identify him as such. A second possibility is that the figure represents the culture hero Bochica, a figure who looms large in Muisca lore. Given the importance of the culture hero as avatar of the solar deity in other Colombian cultures, it would be surprising if Bochica were not represented in the art of the Muisca. A third possibility is that the personage represents an ideal type such as priest or ruler.

Chieftain jars, as they are popularly called, are the most common form of anthropomorphized vessel in the Late Tairona art of the Sierra Nevada de Santa Marta. Typically, the vessel is characterized by a distinct base, body, neck, and rim. The base may be a simple straight sided or sloping ring. The vessel body, which doubles as the figure's body, takes the form of a globular chamber. The neck of the vessel is usually modeled and serves as the head (cat. no. 106). The nose and accompanying nose plaque are usually prominent, but ears and other facial details are often only slightly indicated. Sometimes the figure is adorned with a lip plug.

The head is often distinguished from the body of the vessel by a narrow indentation that serves as the neck. Feet are not portrayed in true chieftain jars. Arms and hands are normally foreshortened and either rendered in relief or as appliqués. The figure may or may not wear a necklace or pendant. When a pendant is indicated, it is usually in the form of an eagle, a bird closely associated with the sun and shamanism in Tairona iconography.

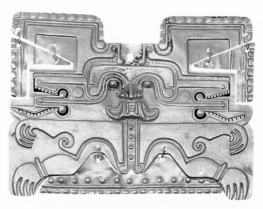

66.

EAR ORNAMENTS WITH SHAMANIC FIGURE

The ornaments are formed of sheet metal and decorated using the repoussé technique. The face and limbs of the central figure are rendered in relief. The technical mastery evidenced in these artworks is of the highest order. The details of the openwork elements are rendered with a precision difficult to attain even with modern steel-chasing tools, according to metals expert Robert Sonin (personal communication).

The central figure of each ornament is a fanged, winged, anthropomorphic creature, who likely represents an empowered, transformed shaman in soul flight. *Tingunas* in the form of stylized dragon heads can be seen at the side of each head. The arms have been transformed into wings while the face is more like that of a jaguar than a human being. The iconography is overwhelmingly shamanic in intent. Department of Valle del Cauca. Late Ilama or Malagana style. Ca. 200 B.C.-A.D. 200. Gold. (A) 4⅜" h. x 5⅝" w.; (B) 4⅜" h. x 5¾" w. Private collection

STANDING SHAMAN

The "dragon" heads at each side of the head of the central figure represent *tingunas*, emanations of vital force, indicative of shamanic power. The figure holds a cylindrical object of unknown significance in each hand. The headdress is composed of a band of alternating upward and downward pointing triangles, a geometric configuration associated with concepts of fertility. Department of Valle del Cauca. Late Ilama or Malagana style. Ca. 200 B.C.-A.D. 200. Gold. 2⅝" h. Private collection

67.

ANTHROPOMORPHIC PECTORAL

ANTHROPO-ZOOMORPHIC PECTORAL

Eagle pendants identical to those seen on chieftain jars were cast in gold or tumbaga, a copper-gold alloy (cat. no. 153).

The iconography associated with the chieftain jars is very similar to that of Tairona *ocarinas* with figures seated on a bench (cat. no. 13). It is likely that both the chieftain jars, as well as *ocarinas*, portray the same personage but perhaps in slightly different aspects. For example, the chieftain jar figures lack the large radiating headdresses characteristic of the *ocarinas*. As previously noted, the iconography associated with the *ocarinas* fits the ethnographic descriptions of the Kogi solar deity who sits in the heavens, radiating his life force in order to engender, nourish, and sustain life on earth.

The solar deity has another aspect. He comes to earth as avatar, the culture hero who teaches mankind the civilizing arts and sciences. As with so much native myth, profound esoteric truth hides behind disarmingly quaint and seemingly naive metaphor. To apprehend the truths we must penetrate the veil of metaphor.

In this instance, the sun, as culture hero, begins his journey as illuminating rays of sunlight. It is in the form of solar rays that his aspect as avatar is assumed. In the art, however, divinity is given human form. The light of the sun not only fertilizes the earth, it also fertilizes the human mind through its power of illumination. In the light of day the relationship of one thing to another is revealed.

Without sunlight not only is life at risk but also seeing and understanding are impaired. It is in his capacity as illuminator that the solar deity is perceived as culture hero and teacher. After all, the solution to problems lies in our ability to see problems clearly. Light facilitates seeing, seeing leads to understanding, and understanding promotes the arts and sciences. In English, the associations between light and understanding are clear—illuminate, elucidate, enlighten. The word *divinity* is derived from the Indo-European root *div*,

ANTHROPOMORPHIC PECTORAL (PRECEDING PAGES)

68. Rendered in a schematized manner, the figure represents a composite creature with human and animal characteristics. The use of matched geometric stepped frets to represent the arms and legs is typical of the Tolima style. The composition represents an empowered, transformed shaman. Indigenous concepts of duality are encoded in the portrayal. Opposing rectilinear elements atop the head contrast with the curvilinear turned-in elements forming the end of the tail. The arms and legs also oppose yet complement one another. This composition emphasizes the shaman's role as mediator of the positive and negative, male and female forces that underlie all phenomena. Middle Magdalena River region. Tolima style. A.D. 200-1600. Gold. 11¼" h. x 5⅞" w. Museo del Oro (5833)

ANTHROPO-ZOOMORPHIC PECTORAL (PRECEDING PAGES)

69. This composition blends avian and human characteristics, although the avian characteristics predominate. The representation is that of a transformed shaman in "soul flight." Shamans were believed capable of flying about in their "soul." While in soul flight the shaman's physical body would remain in a preserved, motionless condition. Middle Magdalena River region. Tolima style. A.D. 200-1600. Gold. 7⅞" h. x 3⅜" w. Museo del Oro (6235)

which means light. The solar deity as culture hero is probably the personage portrayed in the so-called chieftain jars. As the large Late Tairona anthropomorphic funerary urns (cat. no. 98) are little more than schematized large chieftain jars, they may also represent this personage, who may have served as a model for earthly rulers.

Surviving prehistoric masks are rare

in the art of prehispanic Colombia. Most of those actually used in ritual were undoubtedly made of perishable materials such as wood or fiber, as they are even today in Colombia's surviving indigenous cultures. Those that have survived are made of gold or fired clay. Stone masks are extremely rare. Surviving masks have almost without exception been recovered from graves.

Why were these masks made? And why were they placed in graves? Any attempt to interpret such masks must rely on careful observation and study of contextual iconography, which may help identify whom or what the mask represents and how it functioned. Those few individuals graced with a mask in death clearly enjoyed high status within their respective cultures. Status usually, though not necessarily, correlates with material wealth. We should therefore expect to find masks, particularly gold ones, in association with other grave goods of an elite nature. In fact, this is precisely the case with virtually all gold masks that have been excavated. Unfortunately, similar corroboration is lacking for the majority of pottery masks.

Gold was valued not as a monetary medium but because of its perceived religious powers. Among the Kogi Indians today, gold is associated with the fertilizing energy of the sun and has the ability to empower the wearer. Gold masks and other objects radiate and exhaust their power and have to be reempowered periodically by exposing them to sunlight. In the past, this renewal usually took place at specific times of year in a sacred spot specially selected for the occasion (Reichel-Dolmatoff 1988).

The ethnohistorical and ethnographic sources inform us that masks were objects associated with either shamans, priests, or rulers, who sometimes were the same individual. Masks not only conceal but also reveal. The face and persona of the wearer of a mask is hidden and subordinated to the personage portrayed in the mask. Personality is little more than a mask projected onto the world knowingly or unknowingly by the inner self. The English word *personality* is ultimately derived from the Latin word *persona*, which

ANTHROPOMORPHIC PENDANT
The shoulders, breasts, and arms are configured in the form of a feline head. The eyes of the feline are formed by the breasts of the human figure. Department of Valle del Cauca. Late Ilama or Malagana style. Ca. 200 B.C.-A.D. 200. Gold. 1⅛" h. x ⅜" w. Private collection

71.

referred to masks worn by actors in Roman drama meaning "that through which sound passes." In prehispanic Nahuatl-speaking Mexico the idiom "to create a face" meant to cultivate character, depth, and substance in one's personality. In English one speaks of "saving face," meaning safeguarding the projected image of oneself. The human face projects identity, as well as state of mind.

A few empirical observations on Colombian masks should be noted. For one thing, the majority of full-sized masks in either gold or clay are found in the more southerly regions of the country—Nariño, Tierradentro, Calima, and the Middle Cauca. The majority of Nariño masks are of pottery and are rendered in the Tuza and Tumaco styles, the latter highly variable as compared with other styles. The majority of Tierradentro, Calima, and Middle Cauca masks are of gold. Most Calima masks, whether clay or gold, are in the Ilama style.

Some of the portrayals in clay were standardized, forming recurrent genres. Catalogue number 123, an example of a recurrent genre in the Tuza style of Highland Nariño, is characterized by a long face with half-closed eyes, a distinct M-shaped hairline that frames the face, and a bulge in the cheek that presumably represents a wad of coca leaf. This composition is the most frequently encountered clay mask in the Tuza style. The artist has emphasized the bulge in the cheek and the mental state induced by chewing coca leaf. To judge by the half-closed eyes and facial demeanor, the result is inner calm and silent contemplation.

In a second mask rendered in this style (cat. no. 122), four figures adorn the top of the mask, but it retains the distinctive Tuza-style hairline framing the face. Each of the four

SHAMAN HOLDING BATONS
The term Darien was formerly applied to specific genres of goldwork found over wide areas of northern and central Colombia, as well as Central America. It is extremely unusual to find examples in clay. This composition represents a standing priest or shaman officiate holding a baton or staff in each hand. The two bosses seen atop the head are schematized, abstracted elements that in some compositions represent the double-spouted vessel form called *alcarraza*; and in others, represent mushrooms. Northern Colombia region. Style and date unknown. Buff pottery. 5⅜" h. x 4⅛" w. Museo del Oro (CS12794)

73.

PENDANT IN THE FORM OF A PRIEST OR SHAMAN
Pendants such as this are found widely distributed in Colombia from the Tolima region of the Middle Magdalena to the Caribbean coast. The figures are invariably highly abstract and often scarcely discernible. The eyes are barely visible behind the spiral ornaments held in front of the figure's face. In some examples, the disc-shaped ornaments atop the head are clearly represented as *alcarrazas*, while in others they are shaped like mushrooms. The spiral ornaments held in front of the face complement the spiral ornamentation seen along each side of the figure's head. The figure's hands are rendered as little more than lugs. The legs and feet are wide and flat with open space between each leg. The figure likely represents a shaman-priest in ritual garb. The spiral ornaments may symbolize growth, possibly of plant life. Northern Colombia region. Style and date unknown. Gold. 4½" h. x 3¾" w. Museo del Oro (6419). Publications: Labbé, ed., 1992, cover; Bray 1978, cat. no. 253.

72.

74.

surmounting figures holds a large cylindrical jar. Below the figures is a band of painted geometrics consisting of parallel chevrons, a pattern that for many indigenous cultures symbolizes running water. The paired perforated discs attached to the sides of the front of the mask are an unusual characteristic of this mask. They are awkwardly positioned to have served only to fasten the mask to the wearer. Possibly they also served to hold decorations like feathers or stalks of vegetation.

The iconography suggests the mask may have been used in rain-making rituals. The band of chevrons below the four figures implies they are pouring water from their jars. If so, the poured water produces a flowing stream.

An unusual rectangular pottery mask is rendered in a style reminiscent of faces of column sculptures found in some of the large underground chambered tombs (e.g., Loma de Segovia) of the Tierradentro region. It is characterized by a horizontal bar of appliquéd clay that serves as the brow ridge. A second bar of appliqué serves as the nose (cat. no. 120). Pinched appliqués are used for the eyes and mouth. The face has a sad, forlorn appearance.

A unique mask in Tumaco-La Tolita style portrays a face looking sharply to the side (cat. no. 124). The effect is created by filling the right half of each hollow eye socket with clay. The ears are adorned with earspools, the nose with a nose ring. The upper lip is curved in such a way as to impart a sense of apprehension.

Only a few clay masks from the Calima region are known. All are rendered in a genre within the Ilama style. Although each example is somewhat distinctive in shape and size, there are certain common characteristics. For example, the face is characterized by numerous wrinkles to depict age. They are either incised (cat. no. 121) or modeled (cat. no. 126). The nose is typically prominent. Sometimes two protrusions can be seen aside and below the mouth (cat. no. 121). The most characteristic wrinkle pattern extends across the forehead, nose, and cheeks,

FIGURAL WHISTLE: PRIEST IN RITUAL ATTIRE

Detailed incised decoration is characteristic of Tairona fine incised brownware. The figure is clothed in highly ornate ritual attire. The distended tongue may identify the personage as the culture hero-avatar aspect of the solar deity or a priest representing this personage. Tairona region. Late Tairona style. Ca. A.D. 1000-1600. Dark brown pottery. 3⅛" h. x 2⅜" w. Private collection

75.

PECTORAL: ANTHROPOMORPHIC FIGURE

The pectoral is formed from hammered and cut sheet metal decorated by repoussé. The distended tongue is reminiscent of representations found in the ceramic art of an elevated personage, likely the solar deity, seated on a bench. Tairona region. Late Tairona style. Ca. A.D. 1000-1600. Gold. 3⅜" h. x 6⅛" w. Museo del Oro (14618). Publications: Bray 1978, no. 308.

ALCARRAZA: STANDING PRIEST OR SHAMAN IN FELINE MASK

76. The contrasting red and white areas are characteristic of the Malagana style. The fanged anthropomorphized personage is a Malagana version of a figure found in other parts of Southwest Colombia. The figure stands on a circular platform in an aggressive, menacing posture. The mouth is fanged and the eyes are placed within the contours of stylized serpents. The figure may represent an empowered shaman ready to engage the forces of evil or other threats. The theme of "shaman in combat" is found in shamanic-based cultures from the north coast of Peru through West Mexico. Department of Valle del Cauca. Malagana style. Ca. 150 B.C.-A.D. 200. Pottery with red and white slip. 9⅜" h. x 5½" w. Private collection. Publications: Archila 1996, pl. 74.

giving the appearance of a crayfish (cat. no. 121) though there may have been no intent to portray this species.

In Mesoamerican iconography, a wrinkled face was associated with the old Lord of Fire, Huehueteotl, who was an avatar of the cosmic dual deity known as Ometeotl. Another of his iconographic traits is a mouth with only two teeth, which symbolizes both his own dual nature and his relationship to the cosmic dual deity. It is tempting to see in this mask from Calima a reflection of concepts found far to the north in Mesoamerica. Unfortunately, there are no contemporary ethnographic groups from the Calima region to guide us in validating our suspicions.

The majority of surviving gold masks come from the Calima region (cat. nos. 129, 130) and other parts of Southwest Colombia. Although most of the Calima and Cauca masks are in the Ilama style, a few are rendered in the Late Ilama or Malagana style (cat. no. 128). Most were crafted from sheet gold that has been cut and hammered into the desired shape. Decoration was effected using repoussé. Often danglers are attached to the mask with gold staples.

Other gold masks (cat. no. 128) are shaped like solar discs. Since gold is closely associated with the sun over wide areas of the Americas, it is likely that at least some of these masks represent the solar deity.

A gold Yotoco-style pectoral (cat. no. 127) from the Calima region also suggests iconographic concepts found far to the north in Mesoamerica. The pectoral is in the form of a cleft plaque with a head at the center adorned with large earspools. The face is hidden behind a large feline mask that serves as a nose ornament. Two bands decorated with birds, geometrics, and other iconography emerge from behind the head of the central figure. Each band flows in opposite directions to the right and left but actually is one unified band.

This composition is reminiscent of the so-called Aztec calendar stone, which has the face of Tonatiuh, the solar deity, at its center. Two streams of energy in serpent form emerge from Tonatiuh and flow to the right and left. They come together at the base of the

FIGURAL WHISTLE: PRIEST IN RITUAL ATTIRE

The monumentality of this small figural sculpture is characteristic of Tairona art. The image of an anthropomorphic feline suggests a shamanic figure is intended. Powerful shamans were said to be able to transform their vital force spirit to take on the appearance of a jaguar. Tairona region. Late Tairona style. Ca. A.D. 1000-1600. Grey-brown pottery. 4 ½" h. x 3 ⅜" w. Museo del Oro (CT1038)

78.

CANASTERO: SEATED MALE FIGURE

Every line in this composition exemplifies the artist's mastery of the medium. The pyramidal, triangular configuration of the upper body is mirrored in the configuration of the lower body. A similar symmetry prevails between the right and left sides of the body. The figure is seated in a composed meditative posture. The S-scroll incised decoration on the torso likely represents tattooing. Calima region. Ilama style. Ca. 1000 B.C.-A.D. 1. Pottery with brown slip. 9 ⅞" h. x 2 ⅞" w. Private collection. Publications: Labbé 1986, pl. 7; Labbé 1988, pl. 7.

79.

81.

ALCARRAZA: SEATED FIGURE

One of the many interpretations of this composition is that the figure is extracting a splinter from the sole of the foot. It is also possible that the posture has some shamanic significance, given the preponderant shamanic context of much prehispanic art from Colombia. Department of Valle del Cauca. Malagana style. Ca. 150 B.C.-A.D. 200. Pottery with red and white slip. 6⅛" h. x 6" w. Private collection. Publications: Archila 1996, pl. 47.

82.

KNEELING FEMALE FIGURE

The oversized head and prominent genitalia are typical of female figures in this style. The eyes are coffee-bean shaped and the mouth is formed by a single narrow groove. Incising is used to indicate body decoration, and punctating is used as infill within geometric forms and to delineate the pubic area. Kneeling on one knee is not common in the art of Colombia. Caribbean Lowlands. Style and date unknown. Cream-brown pottery. 10¾" h. x ⅞" w. Museo del Oro (CS12823)

SQUATTING FIGURE WITH GOLD EARRINGS

80. Typical of the llama style are the broad shoulders, massive body, and large flat feet. The fine crosshatched decoration atop the head and along the necklace are characteristic of llama ceramic art from the Calima region. The *canastero*, like the *alcarraza*, was a vessel form used by the Calima artists to communicate shared cultural themes. The naked male in a squatting posture is a stock theme in llama art. This composition may represent a shaman singing a power song, and the position may represent one assumed by llama shamans while engaged in this activity. In controlled excavations figural pottery sculptures are sometimes found adorned with gold jewelry such as this. When found by treasure hunters the gold ornaments are generally removed and sold separately. Calima region. llama style. 1000 B.C.-A.D. 1. Pottery with traces of brown slip, and gold earrings. 14" h. x 14" w. (earrings, 2⅜" h.) Museo del Oro (CC1857, 9048, 9049)

103.

composition in the form of a butterfly pattern that symbolizes their inherent union and fertilizing power. The two streams represent the male and female aspects of the sacred energy (*teotl*), the effluence and essence of the solar deity. He is, like Hueheteotl, the Lord of Fire, an avatar of the cosmic deity Ometeotl.

In the Colombian pectoral the feline nose mask may represent the sun in its night aspect, typically symbolized by the jaguar, an animal closely associated with shamans, darkness, caves, fire, and the sun. A row of dots line the lower edge of the bands. Commonly used as a seed symbol in Colombia, the dots further accentuate the fertilizing power of the energy emitted by the solar deity. Indeed, the Kogi Indians of northern Colombia speak of sunlight as the semen or seed of the sun.

ZOOMORPHIC REPRESENTATIONS

Profuse in the art of prehispanic

Colombia, animal imagery is used in a variety of contexts as symbol, metaphor, and allegory. Animals were represented realistically, stylistically, or in fantastic guise. They were portrayed, in whole or in part, as central figures of a composition or as subordinates. Animals could be anthropomorphized by giving them human attributes like hands and feet (cat. no. 142), or the human form could be zoomorphized by giving it animal characteristics such as fangs, claws, or tail (cat. no. 146).

Certain forms such as birds were common to all regions and styles while other forms were used only by some. Occasionally a specific animal is closely associated with a particular artifact. For example, the butterfly is commonly represented in Tairona nose plaques (cat. no. 155) while birds and frogs are the preferred species in small Tairona gold rattles.

Sinú gold staff finials are usually in the form of birds, felines, deer, or crocodilians. In the art of Nariño, felines in clay are sculpted in the round, while Nariño deer in the Tuza style are rendered as painted design on the interior of footed bowls (cat. no. 167). Depictions of frogs are widespread, but toads are most common in the clay art of the Calima

SEATED SHAMAN

The composition consists of a seated male with arms engulfing and holding the knees, a recurrent theme in Muisca goldwork. According to contemporary Tukano shamans (Reichel-Dolmatoff 1988, 44), this posture is assumed when the shaman enters a trance state in order to heighten awareness. There are many examples of this genre in the Museo del Oro's collection. In most examples, the mouth is depicted open, suggesting the chanting of a power song. Muisca region. Muisca style. Ca. A.D. 900-1600. Gold. 1⅞" h. Museo del Oro (1263). Publications: Reichel-Dolmatoff 1988, cat. no. 19; Bray 1978, cat. no. 341.

83.

WHISTLE: SQUATTING MALE DIGNITARY

The figure is depicted chewing a wad of coca leaf while in a squatting position. The chest plaque, or pectoral, which probably represents one made of gold, is decorated with two interfacing dragons (possibly seahorses) with serpent tails. His foreskin is shown tucked under a penis string, a common element of male attire among many tropical forest cultures of South America. They are depicted in the art of some Tairona groups who lived along the coast. Male nudity among groups in the Amazon who still employ penis strings consists in an exposed glans, not other parts of the male genitalia per se. Tairona region. Late Tairona style. Ca. A.D. 1000-1600. Dark brown pottery. 4½" h. x 3⅞" w. Private collection

84.

PENDANT: STANDING PRIEST OR SHAMAN

SEATED FEMALE FIGURE

region. Moreover, they are usually rendered in the Yotoco style, although rare examples are also found in the earlier Ilama style (cat. no. 144). In Nariño, pottery *ocarinas* in Tuza style were almost exclusively modeled in the form of gastropods, or mollusks.

Given the large number of species available in the regional ecosystems, the limited number selected by the artists is noteworthy. Serpents, frogs, toads, birds, monkeys, armadillos, and bats were the favored species in the gold and ceramic art of the Calima region. Felines were depicted, but usually either in anthropomorphized or mythic forms or, when realistically rendered, in the form of feline heads in ornamental goldwork.

In the Sinú region a variety of birds (usually with long beaks), fish, crocodilians, and felines were preferred. The Tairona bestiary was quite elaborate and included eagles, frigates, pelicans, long-beaked birds, bats, butterflies, frogs, felines, serpents, crocodilians, and opossums.

The Muisca inventory was more abbreviated. Serpents, felines, frogs, and insects were cast in gold and tumbaga, fish sometimes carved in stone, and serpents seen mainly as added or painted decoration on pottery vessels.

The predominant species in Nariño included birds, deer, monkeys, frogs, lizards, snails, and other gastropods as well as jaguars. In Tumaco-La Tolita pottery, animal forms are almost exclusively sculpted in the round and include birds, fish and sharks, jaguars, and, very rarely, domestic dogs. Undoubtedly, specific animals represent particular aspects of indigenous shamanic ideology or were used as characters in native myth and allegory.

Conjoined or paired animal representations are most common in cultures from northern Colombia, such as the Malamboid (cat. nos. 132, 133, 136, 137), Naguanje (cat. no. 139), and

87.
SEATED CHANTING FEMALE
The arms and shoulders are rendered in relief and are proportionately thin. The figure appears to be pregnant and is depicted seated with mouth wide open, suggesting that she is chanting a power song, which is somehow related to her pregnancy. Highland Nariño region, Department of Nariño. Capulí style. Ca. A.D. 850-1500. Pottery with red slip and resist decoration. 8¾" h x 5¼" w. Private collection.

85.
PENDANT: STANDING PRIEST OR SHAMAN (PRECEDING PAGES)
Despite its diminutive size, the figure has monumental qualities. The proportionately massive shoulders repeat a trait found in Malagana ceramic figures. Representing a shaman or priest performing a chant, the figure holds a baton in each hand, seemingly striking one against the other to keep cadence. Department of Valle del Cauca. Late Ilama or Malagana style. Ca. 200 B.C.-A.D. 200. Gold. 1⁵⁄₁₆" h. Private collection

86.
SEATED FEMALE FIGURE (PRECEDING PAGES)
The body is essentially columnar with little distinction made between the head and the torso. A shallow groove serves as the neck. Typically, the limbs are formed of long cylindrical rolls of clay, with little emphasis on toes or fingers. Figures such as this constitute a genre of Middle Cauca sculpture characterized by crossed legs and seated posture. The artist has captured a sense of deep repose and serenity, qualities highly esteemed and idealized in prehispanic Colombia. Middle Cauca region. Late Quimbaya style. Ca. A.D. 1000-1600. Pottery with red slip, red paint, resist decoration, and gold nose ring. 15" h. x 9" w. Private collection

Late Tairona (cat. no. 134), and occasionally in other regional cultures, such as the Ilama of the Calima region (cat. no. 131).

Even though conjoined, the two heads are often intentionally unequal. In catalogue number 137, for example, each head is distinct. In the Naguanje example (cat. no. 139) the head with spout is both larger and positioned higher than the other. Such artistic conventions accentuate both the separateness of each aspect and the unity of the overall form. These compositions reflect the indigenous understanding of the duality inherent in nature, as explained previously.

A number of compositions confront us with fantastic creatures not found in the real world (cat. nos. 141, 142, 144). These may represent figures taken from myth or allegory or shamans who have shape-shifted and assumed animal form.

In a Tumaco-La Tolita example (cat. no. 142) the arms and legs are distinctly human while the wings and large triangular head give the figure the appearance of an anthropomorphic fly. The composition may represent a shaman in transformation—the wings suggesting soul flight.

The bird-man motif is relatively common in the metal art of Colombia. Certain winged anthropomorphized animals also represent shamans in soul flight.

A unique composition in the Ilama style, an anthropomorphic frog riding a toad (cat. no. 144), appears shamanic in nature. The toad, whose parotid glands are clearly and prominently depicted, appears to be *Bufo marinus*, a species that carries the powerful toxin bufotenine in its skin and even more so in its parotid glands. In small doses this toxin has strong hallucinogenic properties.

GOURD-SHAPED VESSEL
The color and decorative scheme of this vessel is similar to that of Capulí complex wares from the highland region of Nariño. The decoration is laid out in bands of repeating geometric design elements. Although shaped like a gourd, the sculpture is reminiscent of anthropomorphic and zoomorphic figures with mouth open, suggesting the singing of a power song to the forces of the sky for rain or other bounty. Middle Magdalena River region. Early Tolima style. A.D. 200-1000. Pottery with red slip and resist decoration. 8 7/8" h. x 10 1/2" w. Museo del Oro (CTo13034)

88.

Viewed within the context of neotropical shamanism, the composition comes into focus, at least hypothetically. The anthropomorphic frog represents a shaman who has experienced soul body transformation. He has been transported into a visionary experience induced by the powerful mind-altering chemical bufotenine obtained from the toad *Bufo marinus.*

As we have seen frequently, the significance of pre-Columbian imagery is often anything but apparent. A case in point is a zoomorphic cayman dish in Malamboid style (cat. no. 159). A stylized animal's head and tail are readily identified, but only the flattened, straight-edged snout informs us that a crocodilian rather than a turtle is intended. Closer

fig. 4

inspection reveals stylized heads seen in profile and arranged in opposing pairs at each side of the vessel along the rim. Incised S-scrolls flank each of the stylized heads (fig. 5). Four grooved elements extend beyond the rim.

Viewed against the backdrop of pre-Columbian art and science, this composition assumes astronomical significance. The head, tail, and knobs between the profile heads mark off the four cardinal directions. The grooved extensions mark the rising and setting points of the summer and winter solstices. The profile heads represent the movement of the sun along the horizon. During the year, the sun seems to rise in a different place along the eastern horizon each day with the exception of the winter and summer solstices, when it appears to rise at the same point for more than a day. When it begins to move again, it alters its course in the opposite direction. The southernmost point of the sun's journey marks the winter solstice; and the northernmost, the summer solstice. The spring and autumn equinoxes are midway between the two at due east. In pre-Columbian art the daily movement of the sun was imaged either as a circle with a cross superimposed on it to represent the horizon and the four cardinal directions or as an elliptic with the four cardinal points indicated. A circle with cross and superimposed X was used to indicate the horizon, cardinal directions, and solstice points (fig. 5).

ALCARRAZA: CHANTING ZOOMORPH

The vessel is a double-bodied variant of the basic *alcarraza* form. Usually there are two spouts. The mouth of the zoomorphic figure may have served as a spout. In this composition one chamber is in the form of a standing zoomorphic figure generally identified as a bat-man. His mouth is open as if he is chanting. The composition may represent a transformed shaman singing a power song. Department of Valle del Cauca. Malagana style. Ca. 150 B.C.-A.D. 200. Pottery with red and white slip. 7½" h. x 5⅛" w. Private collection. Publications: Archila 1996, pl. 40.

89.

STANDING SHAMAN-MUSICIAN (FOLLOWING PAGES)

The figure represents a priest or shaman in ritual attire. He wears a curled nose ornament and holds a rattle in the right hand and what may be a two-pipe flute in the left. Provenance unknown. Classic Quimbaya style. A.D. 0-800. Gold. 2" h. x 1⅜" w. Museo del Oro (8000). Publications: Reichel-Dolmatoff 1988, cat. no. 46.

90.

ALCARRAZA: SHAMAN WITH ALTER-EGO (FOLLOWING PAGES)

The contrasting white and red colors and the bulbous shoulders of the primary figure are characteristic of the Malagana style. A masked standing figure plays a drum. An eerie figure, partly anthropomorphized, stands behind the masked figure and holds onto his hips. The secondary figure is also attached to the primary figure at the shoulders. The primary figure's mask covers the whole head and is characterized by large circular eye holes. The composition portrays the enactment of a ritual. The secondary figure may represent the primary figure's alter-ego or a spirit ally in animal guise. Department of Valle del Cauca. Malagana style. Ca. 150 B.C.-A.D. 200. Pottery with red and white slip. 9⅜" h. x 5½" w. Private collection. Publications: Archila 1996, pl. 66; Rojas de Perdomo 1995, 191.

91.

STANDING SHAMAN-MUSICIAN

ALCARRAZA: SHAMAN WITH ALTER-EGO

If our interpretation is correct, the head in the Malamboid composition marks off the south, the tail the north—that is, the zenith and nadir of the daily movement of the sun, respectively. The east is on the right side of the composition, marked by the knob between the two profile heads. The profile head facing north—that is, in the direction of the tail—indicates that the sun is moving northward on the eastern horizon toward the summer solstice. The opposing head represents the sun moving southward. The northern grooved element represents sunrise at the summer solstice while the opposite grooved element in the direction of the head represents the winter solstice.

The S-scrolls repeat the pattern of the motion of the sun while the small incised circles on each side of the S-scroll may represent the sun moving along its path. Note that at the equinox point only one circle is inscribed and is positioned in direct alignment with the cardinal point marked by the knob. This circle represents the sun and its position on the eastern horizon for both the spring and autumn equinoxes.

The circle-cross-X pattern was used widely in the Americas to depict the horizon, cardinal directions, and rising and setting points of the solstices on the horizon. What is unusual in the Malamboid example is the presumed early age of this composition and its association with the cayman for the composition is most often associated with the turtle elsewhere in the Americas (see Labbé 1995, for Panamanian examples of this theme).

ALCARRAZA: SHAMAN WITH ANIMAL AT BACK

The curved configuration seen atop the figure's head is an iconographic element also found on some gold figures in Malagana style. The composition likely represents a chanting shaman accompanied by his alter-ego or animal familiar. The object in the hands may be a flute. Department of Valle del Cauca. Malagana style. Ca. 150 B.C.-A.D. 200. Pottery with red slip. 3⅜" h. x 3½" w. Private collection

93.

FIGURE SEATED ON A BENCH

92.

The slit eyes with slightly puffy eyelids, the large nose, and the bulging calves show stylistic affinities with the Late Quimbaya style of the Middle Cauca region. The open mouth with bared teeth is reminiscent of some figures in Malagana style. The figure is seated on a bench with a shield or large disc attached to his left arm. His diadem or headgear is in the form of an anthropomorphic head with radiating crown. At the back of the seated figure is a crested zoomorphic figure with curled tail. This figure likely represents the shamanic alter-ego of the seated figure. The interlocking triangles on both the shield and the crown of the anthropomorphic head connote fertility. There is little doubt that the composition is shamanic in nature. Among many groups in Colombia, the solar deity is perceived to be the First Shaman. The associated iconography on both the shield and crown of the anthropomorphic head are reminiscent of iconography associated with the sun in other regions. It is possible, therefore, that the composition is a portrayal of the solar deity as First Shaman. Popayán region, Department of Valle del Cauca. Popayán style. Date unknown. Buff pottery with traces of red paint. 15" h. x 9" w. x 12½" d. Denver Art Museum; given in memory of Alan Lapiner by Mr. and Mrs. Edward M. Strauss (1977.62). Publications: Labbé 1986, no. 81.

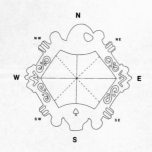

fig. 5

SCHEMATIZED DRAWING
of catalog number 159
indicating the cross
(solid lines on interior of bowl)
and superimposed X
(broken lines on the interior
of bowl) marking off the
four cardinal directions and
solstice sunrise and
sunset points, respectively.
Drawing by
Joseph Kramer.

Astronomical themes are also found in the graphic art of Highland Nariño. In an example in Tuza style (cat. no. 167), the interior of a footed bowl is decorated with a band of animals, cross-shaped elements, and a central tondo or circle with an eight-point "star" at the center. The eight-point star is used even today by indigenous groups like the Pasto as a symbol for the sun. The cross-shaped element is commonly used to represent a star. A reading of the context of the composition would seem to imply that the band of felines and deer are associated with events in the upper world, the sky-world. This reading is implied by the cross-elements as star symbols. Nor is the procession of animals arbitrary: felines alternate with deer; that is, predator with prey. Also, the felines are unusual since all but one have birds on their back. Perhaps they represent transformed shamans, the birds their animal auxiliaries. Since deer were hunted in prehistoric times, the composition may involve concepts pertaining to the role of the shaman in maintaining the bounty of the biosphere and the proliferation of species. In parts of South America only male deer were hunted. The large antlers imply male deer. As guardians of fertility, shamans are mediators between hunters and prey. In parts of the northwest Amazon, the shaman contacts a supernatural personage known as the Master of Animals and entreats him to allow the hunters to kill the intended prey. In native culture, the killing of animals is believed to be serious but necessary. Only ritual and a respectful attitude toward the victim protect the hunter and his group from harm, illness, or even death, which may result as a consequence of his action.

Neotropical shamanism offers the best hope for developing an interpretive framework from which to view the significant body of prehispanic Colombian material culture now housed in the world's museums. The approach to this impressive living database, however, must be multidisciplinary, methodical, and cautious.

Archaeological material culture has traditionally been viewed, particularly by archaeologists, as a resource yielding technological data such as chronologies, provenance,

DRUM

The color scheme and the use of incising suggest that this drum belongs to the Tuza Complex of Highland Nariño. The interlocking crooks, triangles, and other geometric forms are part of a widespread geometric tradition found from the American Southwest through Chile. In those areas where we have ethnographic data concerning native interpretations of these geometric elements there is a surprising degree of similarity. Interfacing and interlocking geometric forms usually connote duality, complementarity, and fertility. Highland Nariño region, Department of Nariño. Tuza style. Ca. A.D. 1250-1500. Pottery with tan and red slip. 8½" h. x 6⅛" w. Michael C. Carlos Museum, Emory University, Atlanta; gift of William C. and Carol W. Thibadeau (1990.11.17)

94.

material composition, manufacturing techniques, and typologies. These in turn have been used to recreate structural and quantifiable dimensions of culture such as house types, site use, site distributions, population density, settlement patterns, gender specific functions, trade, material technology, social organization, ranking, and the like. On the other hand, attempts to interpret less tangible aspects of culture such as religious beliefs, worldviews, cultural values, or esotericism have been few and far between and have been viewed with skepticism by more traditionally oriented investigators.

Such skepticism developed in an era when little scientific ethnography had been undertaken and access to existing documentation was impeded by the realities of late nineteenth- and early twentieth-century scholarship and technology. Today's investigator is confronted with veritable mountains of data that can be readily accessed, in large measure, from a desktop computer. Moreover, the same material culture can be studied from many different perspectives.

Increasingly, multidisciplinary approaches to the same database have proved mutually beneficial. We are rapidly approaching an era when iconographically rich artifacts may soon be read like so much text, albeit imbued with its own peculiar syntax and grammar. In rediscovering the rich legacy that was prehispanic Colombia, perhaps we too will rediscover an aspect of our own humanity, buried in a time when the world was filled with shamans, gods, and mythic beasts.

BOWL WITH PAINTED FIGURES

Tuza-style painted bowls reflect an art tradition found widely dispersed in the Americas from the American Southwest down through Chile. The tradition is characterized by a common body of geometric design elements, design layouts, and in some cases themes. The design on the interior of the bowls is characterized by a circular tondo encircled by one or more decorative bands. An eight-point star, representing either the sun or the planet Venus, lies at the center of the bowl within the tondo. The primary decorative band consists of a circle of figures holding hands. The "tunics" of the figures are decorated with pairs of white and red triangles. These form butterfly patterns, symbols of fertility emblematic of shamans in their role as guardians of fertility and mediators of the biosphere. The theme is identical to one found on painted bowls from the American Southwest. The figures with joined hands may represent the chain of being, which depends on the life-giving rays of the solar deity. On a more prosaic level, the figures may be interpreted as participating in a circle dance. Highland Nariño region, Department of Nariño. Tuza style. Ca. A.D. 1250-1500. Pottery with red paint on white slip. 4¼" h. x 7½" d. Private collection

96.

SHAMAN ATOP A BIRD

95.

The composition is a stock theme in Tairona art. This example may represent a fragment of a larger work that usually includes four such elements attached to the body of a large bird (see Reichel-Dolmatoff 1988, cover). The figure, probably a shaman, is seated atop the head of a long-beaked bird and stares forward with knees clasped tightly as if in a trance. The clasping of the knees may be the Tairona version of a similar posture depicted in Muisca goldwork and still assumed by Tukano shamans of the Northwest Amazon. Tairona region. Late Tairona style. Ca. A.D. 1000-1600. Gold. 2½" h. x 1⅛" w. Museo del Oro (26177)

THE MALAGANA CHIEFDOM,

A NEW DISCOVERY IN THE

CAUCA VALLEY OF SOUTHWESTERN COLOMBIA

BY WARWICK BRAY, LEONOR HERRERA, AND MARIANNE CARDALE SCHRIMPFF

THE PREHISTORY

of the Cauca Valley has for a long time been something of a mystery. Although the valley was described as one of the most fertile and beautiful places on earth by the German scientist Baron Alexander von Humboldt when he visited in the early years of the last century, it had apparently remained uninhabited until relatively recently, in spite of its exceptional attractions. A number of archaeologists carried out intensive surveys and excavations in different areas of the valley but found sites only of the latest period, the Sonsoid, which dates from about A.D. 800 to the Spanish conquest (Ford 1944; Cubillos 1984; Rodríguez 1992). The one exception was the work of Bray and Moseley (1971), who defined a pre-Sonsoid style, nowadays called Yotoco, in their excavations near the city of Buga.

ANTHROPOMORPHIC FUNERARY URN

97. This urn form, unique to the Middle Magdalena region, lacks the neck and decorated lids of other Magdalena burial urns. Pubenza polychrome urns, although superficially shaped like the Chimila urns far to the north, lack the bases found on Chimila urns. Additionally, faces are placed on the shoulders of the vessels rather than on the lids, as in the Chimila style. The color schemes of the two styles are also different. The urn is anthropomorphized by painting and modeling a face on the shoulder of the vessel. Middle Magdalena River region in Tolima. Pubenza polychrome style (Tolima). Ca. A.D. 1000-1400. Buff pottery with red, white, and black paint. 13" h. (base), 2¾" h. (lid). Museo del Oro (Cto-936)

These few sites were all found some distance north of Malagana, close to the foothills of the Western Cordillera. Although some authorities suggested that the apparent absence of earlier sites could be the result of a rapid rate of sedimentation that buried them beneath deep accumulations of silt carried down by the Cauca River and its tributaries, this speculation remains unconfirmed.

This situation changed dramatically in late 1992 when what can only be described as a "treasure" of gold items was offered for sale to the Museo del Oro in Santafé de Bogotá (Archila 1996). According to those who brought the pieces, this remarkable find was made by accident when heavy earth-moving equipment was used to improve the drainage in the sugar-cane fields of the hacienda Malagana near the town of Palmira. Contemporary newspaper reports estimate that five thousand people (from schoolchildren, shopkeepers, and even nuns, to professional treasure hunters) swarmed into the area. Despite the efforts of the army and police force, this invasion resulted in the wholesale destruction of unique archaeological evidence and the nearly complete disappearance of an important chapter of history.

A visitor to the hacienda Malagana today would, at first glance, find little to indicate its former glory. Flat fields, either recently ploughed or covered with dense stands of waving green sugar cane six to ten feet high, reveal no special features, even though those old enough to remember the days before mechanical farming suggest that a few elevated areas or low mounds may once have existed there. However, an inspection of the long drainage ditches that crisscross these fields reveals accumulations of potsherds in their walls. We do not know exactly what the area looked like two thousand years ago, when the settlement at Malagana was at its height, but there was undoubtedly a lot more water, with extensive areas of marshland and lagoons with rich populations of wild duck and other water birds, turtles, fish, and a variety of small mammals. Pollen studies reveal that several species of palm trees grew in the area, and carbonized seeds leave no doubt that Malagana was a flourishing farming community with maize as one of the chief crops. The relatively light soils around the settlement would have been both easy to cultivate and exceptionally fertile.

ANTHROPOMORPHIC JAR

Long fillets of clay enveloping tiny coffee-bean shaped eyes, a nose ring, and a labret are the only indications that this vessel is rendered in human form. Close examination reveals that the lugs of the vessel serve as the arms and the hands of the figure, and that the tiny appliqués arranged in series serve as the figure's necklace. This artwork appears to be a highly stylized representation of a genre of figural jars more commonly found in Tairona black and brownware. Compare this example with catalogue number 106, which is stylistically more exemplary of this genre. Tairona region. Tairona style (cream-colored ware). Ca. A.D. 800-1600. Cream-colored pottery. 7 ⅞" h. Museo del Oro (CT1395)

ANTHROPOMORPHIC FUNERARY URN

99.

Tamalameque-style urns are characterized by lids that incorporate the head, shoulders, and arms of the figure. The body of the urn represents the undifferentiated body of the figure. The dynamic curvilinear designs on the face represent facial painting. Lower Magdalena River region. Tamalameque style. A.D. 800-1500. Buff pottery with white paint on face. 32" h. x 14 ⅝" w. Museo del Oro (Ctam1869). Publications: Bray 1978, no. 582.

The rivers that meander their way through the wide Cauca floodplain have constantly shifted course. At present the site is only a few hundred yards from the Rio Bolo, once a relatively wide river that would have provided a useful waterway for canoe traffic. Some

ten miles downsteam, the Bolo joins the Cauca, which has at all times served as one of Colombia's main north-south arteries for river travel. Since Malagana is situated approximately in the center of the Cauca Valley (fig. 1), a visitor there can enjoy both the misty sunrise over the peaks of the Central Cordillera and the spectacular sunsets over the mountains that separate the valley from the Pacific lowlands to the west.

The first scientific excavations at Malagana were carried out in 1993 by Alvaro Botiva, Eduardo Forero, and David Stemper as part of a joint project funded by the Colombian Institute of Anthropology and the Institute for Scientific Studies in the Department of Valle del Cauca. In the short time that the archaeologists were able to remain in the area, they managed to excavate three graves and uncover a complex and puzzling stratigraphy of settlement (Botiva and Forero 1994).

It was nearly two years after this initial discovery before a group of archaeologists had the opportunity to investigate the site once more (Herrera, Cardale de Schrimpff, and Rodríguez 1994; Rodríguez et al. 1993). The excavations were conducted in an unusual fashion. The site was exceptionally important, and virtually every archaeologist who had worked in Southwestern Colombia contributed a week of their time, a form of cooperation known among the indigenous population of the Southwest as a *minga.*

By this time, sugar cane was growing again over the fields where the destructive activities of the treasure hunters had been most intense. Recalling the almost lunar appearance of this area when looting was at its peak, with huge craters pocking the surface among the irregular dumps of excavated soil, and recognizing that everything had since been flattened by bulldozers, the archaeological team decided to concentrate their efforts at a point some five hundred yards farther off, where there had been much less disturbance.

Over a period of four months, the team[1] excavated an area of some three hundred square yards, uncovering not only seventeen burials but also evidence of four separate periods of occupation, which are named, from earliest to most recent, "Proto-Ilama" (a provisional name), Ilama, Malagana, and Sonsoid.

The most ancient stratum was a compact, well-trodden occupation surface, probably the surface of a low island rising only a foot or so above the marshes that covered much of the surrounding area. There are radiocarbon dates of 300 B.C. ± 50 years and 250 B.C. ±

110 for this occupation, which are later than expected.[2] The fragments of pottery found trodden into the floor were rather different from anything previously known from the region but seemed related to (and possibly ancestral to) the Ilama style—hence the term Proto-Ilama. The Ilama style is already familiar from work in Calima in the neighboring Western Cordillera, where it has been dated to the first millennium B.C. (Cardale de Schrimpff 1992a).

Indeed, after a lapse of time marked by a thick accumulation of clays and other alluvial deposits, people of the typical Ilama culture began living in the excavated area and using pottery identical to the Ilama wares found in Calima. A single radiocarbon date of 290 B.C. ± 60 suggests that this second occupation at Malagana belongs to a late stage of the Ilama period.

It had been clear to all who had seen the initial finds of gold from Malagana that a very strong Ilama influence was present in some items, but the discovery of Ilama occupation at the site came as a surprise. Malagana is the first Ilama settlement to be found outside the mountains of the Western Cordillera and therefore the first indication that the territory of the Ilama people included part of the Cauca Valley.

Unfortunately, both the age of the earlier Proto-Ilama pottery and its precise relationship with the mature Ilama style are difficult to establish. On the one hand, the depth of the alluvium separating the two occupations suggests a considerable difference in age; on the other, the radiocarbon dates for the two periods are surprisingly close together. The contradiction has not yet been resolved.

fig. **3**

DOUBLE-CHAMBERED WHISTLING JAR
from the cemetery at Malagana.
Traces of fine-line negative
painted decoration are visible on the
human figure. Private collection

The Ilama people at Malagana lived on an area of highly fertile but soft, alluvial sands and loams. At the excavation site much of this soil had been disturbed or even totally removed by later occupants, the "Malagana" people who were perhaps the direct descendants of the Ilama population and were contemporary with the Yotoco occupation that followed Ilama in the mountains of Calima.

In fact, a few pieces of Yotoco pottery have been found in the Malagana cemetery. Trade in gold objects between the Cauca Valley and the Cordillera also shows that these two groups of people were in contact with each other. Malagana is a distinct local style, however, that is easily recognizable and unlike anything else known in Colombia.

Most of the radiocarbon dates from the excavations of the Malagana-period occupation fall mainly in the first and second centuries B.C., but the one radiocarbon date from the area where the treasure was found is almost a century later (A.D. 70 ± 60 years) and comes from an enigmatic buried soil, whose context is not entirely clear (Botiva and Forero 1994). Our own excavations, separated from the "treasure zone" by only a short linear distance, may also cover a slightly earlier period of time—possibly the reason why we found no

spectacularly rich burials. Still, it seems unlikely that the two occupations are separated by more than a few generations.

It is, of course, risky to draw firm conclusions from a limited number of radiocarbon dates, especially since we are not yet able to make fine-tuned judgments about the changes in pottery styles. In particular, we do not know exactly when settlement at Malagana began or precisely when it ended. We may be dealing with only a few centuries of occupation or with something much longer—a tradition of pottery-making and goldworking that could span almost a millennium.

So far, there is no indication of any Malagana-period presence after the second century A.D., but one small area of our 1994 excavation produced traces of a Sonsoid reoccupation dating to the last few centuries before the Spanish conquest. Virtually all the remains that might have been left by these final prehispanic occupants of Malagana have vanished, probably destroyed by the heavy earth-moving machinery used to level the area for sugar-cane farming. But less than half a mile away in the neighboring hacienda of Mayajuez, the fields are strewn with Sonsoid sherds, and pottery, graves, and settlements dating to this period have recently been excavated by Rodríguez and Stemper (1994).

ANTHROPOMORPHIC JAR

The form of this figural jar with a single large opening atop the head is one of three vessel forms typical of Ilama ceramics, the other two being the *alcarraza* and *canastero* forms. The closed eyes with puffed eyelids and the sharp downward sloping plane of the lower half of the face are also characteristic of this style. Calima region. Ilama style. Ca. 1000 B.C.-A.D. 1. Pottery with brown slip. 11" h. x 6¼" w. Private collection. Publications: Labbé 1986, no. 43; Labbé 1988, no. 43.

101.

MALE ANTHROPOMORPHIC JAR

Sonso figural jars are exemplary of prehispanic Colombian minimalist art. The basic jar form serves as the head and torso of an abstract human figure. The head is distinguished from the torso by means of a pinch-modeled fillet of clay that frames the face. The arms are not indicated, and the hands are little more than pinch-modeled appliqué discs. The upturned curvature of the mouth is used to give the personage a joyous appearance. The genitalia identify the personage as a male. The artistic intent in this composition may simply have been to impart life and personality to the jar itself rather than portray a specific personage in native myth or cosmology. Calima region. Sonso style. Ca. A.D. 800-1600. Pottery with darkened surface. 14" h. x 8" w. Private collection. Publications: Labbé 1986, no. 61; Labbé 1988, no. 61.

102.

FEMALE ANTHROPOMORPHIC JAR

The artist has used the natural contours of the vessel form to serve as the body of the female. The disproportionately small head, in combination with the ponderous body, large vagina, and bulbous buttocks, suggests that the figure is burdened and vexed by her condition. The tiny arms and hands held aside the head seemingly mock their inadequacy for the task at hand. The composition is probably allegorical in nature. Middle Cauca region. Late Quimbaya style. Ca. A.D. 800-1600. Light brown pottery. 13¼" h. x 11⅜" l. Fondo de Promoción de la Cultura (Q-10825). Publications: *Arte de la Tierra* 1990, no. 5 and cover.

103.

105.

ANTHROPOMORPHIC JAR

The artist has fashioned a vessel in human form in minimalist fashion, with only the head and arms indicated. Typical of the Chimila style are the coffee-bean eyes and appliqué tubular arms made from slender fillets of clay. The figure is holding to its mouth an unidentified object characterized by numerous holes covering its surface. Elevated status is indicated by the large solid gold nose ring, the multiple bracelets at the wrists, and the elaborate hairdo. Department of Magdalena. "Chimila" style. Date unknown. Pottery with tan-colored slip. 15" h. x 12½" w. Private collection

106.

ANTHROPOMORPHIC JAR

The rectilinear qualities of this composition are typical of this genre of figural jars. The arms are appliqués while other details, such as the necklaces and body of the four-headed avian pendant, are rendered in relief. Jars such as this likely represent shaman-priests or the culture hero version of the solar deity. Tairona region. Late Tairona style. Ca. A.D. 1000-1600. Light brown pottery. 9⅜" h. Museo del Oro (CT1334)

MÚCURA WITH ANTHROPOMORPHIC SPOUT

104.

The *múcura*, a globular jar with a tall cylindrical spout used for dispensing liquids, is the quintessential Muisca vessel form. Typically, as in this example, the spout is slightly modified to represent different personages, most likely mythical deities such as the goddess Bachue, who presides over waters and lagoons, or the solar culture hero Bochica. The sex is not specified, but a male figure seems to be intended. Muisca region. Muisca style. Ca. A.D. 900-1600. Pottery with black and red on white slip. 19⅜" h. x 11⅛" w. Museo del Oro (CM-12845)

The discovery of the Malagana cemetery completely changed archaeological perceptions about the history of the Cauca Valley and had interesting repercussions elsewhere. Once archaeologists learned how to recognize Malagana pottery and goldwork, a scattering of old finds in museums and collections fell naturally into place. Soon it became quite clear that Malagana-style items, though unidentified when discovered, had already been found at several sites in the general area.

Among these miscellaneous objects is a clay mask (fig. 2) implausibly reported to come from Guatavita, the sacred lagoon of the Muiscas. When it arrived in Paris in 1891, the mask was acquired by the Musée de l'Homme along with a private collection of Colombian antiquities (Lehmann 1959, pl. 17). For almost a century this piece was considered unique, but it can now be matched with a similar clay mask from a locality close to Malagana.

Further north, but still within the Cauca Valley, a little Malagana-style jar representing a kneeling woman was unearthed near the town of Tuluá, and a particular kind of whistling jar with its front chamber in the form of a human figure has been found sporadically all the way from Caicedonia in the north, just within the boundary of the Quimbaya archaeological zone (Bray 1992, fig. 132), to Tierradentro in the south (Duque Gomez 1979). Vessels identical to these whistling jars in both shape and painted decoration have come from tombs at Malagana (fig. 3), where they are said to be fairly numerous, perhaps an indication that Malagana was the center of manufacture for the group as a whole.

Reappraisal of old collections has also brought to light goldwork of the type found in the Malagana cemetery. One such item is a sheet gold headband or fillet embossed with a

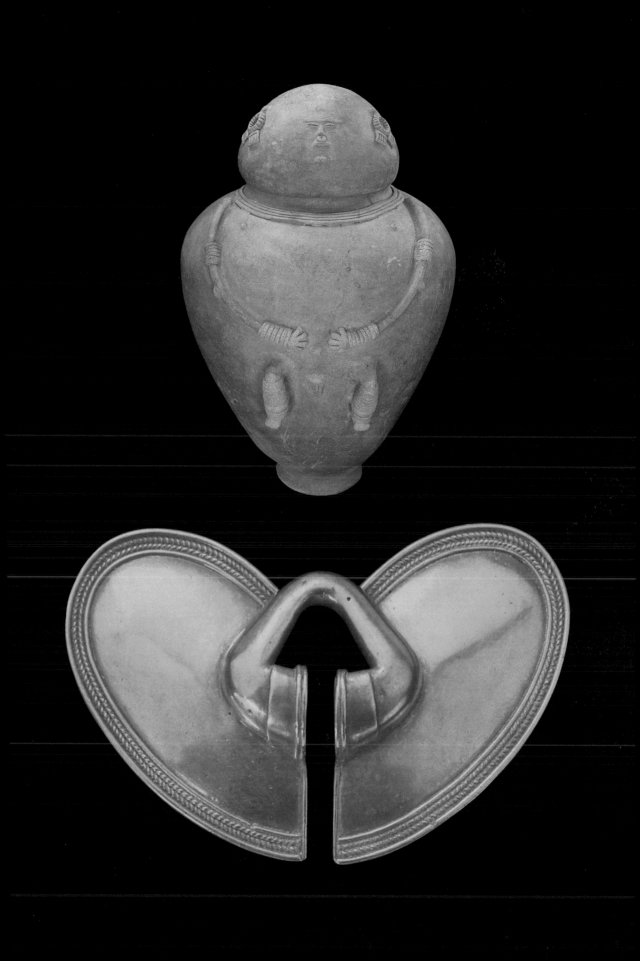

double-headed serpent design (fig. 4). It is said to have been found near Cali, just south of Malagana, and was an early arrival in the Museo del Oro. Another find that predates the discovery of the Malagana cemetery is a little gold statuette, also from the Cauca Valley, that is now in the British Museum (fig. 5).

Casual finds like these show that Malagana was not an isolated site but rather the center of a regional culture with widespread connections. This point is emphasized even more forcefully when we look at the distribution of Malagana gold beads. Individually they are unspectacular, but the sheer quantity and diversity of necklace beads and pendants are unequaled anywhere else in Colombia. Many bead varieties previously thought to have been manufactured in the regions where they were found—for example,

fig. **6**

POTTERY VESSELS
*in the shapes of
houses—from the cemetery
at Malagana.*

the neighboring archaeological zones of Calima, Tolima, and the Upper Magdalena Valley—can be matched among the new finds at Malagana and may have to be reclassified as export pieces from the Cauca Valley.

When we plot all these categories of Malagana pottery and goldwork on a map, they define an "area of contact" that embraces much of the upper Cauca and Magdalena valleys. San Agustín and Tierradentro mark the southern frontier of this zone; its northern boundary falls somewhere near the town of Tuluá, which is close to the southern edge of the Quimbaya archaeological zone. In much of this area the centuries around the time of Christ are still an archaeological blank, and other "Malaganas" may yet be discovered.

Today the Malagana site looks like any other featureless cane field in the Cauca Valley. The people of the floodplain did not build in stone but used perishable materials that do not

FEMALE ANTHROPOMORPHIC BOWL

109. The natural shape of the vessel is deftly integrated with attributes of an essentially female anthropomorphic form. Even though the arms and legs of the figure are rendered in relief, they are elegantly balanced and executed. The coffee-bean eyes are characteristic of a number of Colombian regional styles. The imagery emphasizes the receptiveness and capacity of the personage being portrayed. The contemplative expression of the face may indicate acceptance of her role as receptacle. Probably Middle Cauca region. Classic Quimbaya style. Date unknown. Pottery with black and white paint over a red slip. 4⅜" h. x 9⅝" w. x 13" l. Fondo de Promoción de la Cultura (Q-08766). Publications: Bray 1978, no. 366; *Arte de la Tierra, Colombia: Poder* 1994, no. 51; *Arte de la Tierra* 1990, no. 25.

JAR IN THE FORM OF A HUMAN HEAD

110. The accentuation of the lines depicting eyes, ears, and mouth imparts a penetrating power to what would otherwise be a simple vessel. The partially opened mouth suggests action and movement despite the fact that the vessel is a bodiless head. Calima region. Ilama style. Ca. 1000 B.C.-A.D. 1. Pottery with traces of red-brown slip. 5½" h. x 5¼" w. Private collection

135.

III.

HEAD PENDANT

Rattles shaped like a human head are characteristic of the Lower San Jorge River region.
Similar examples have been found in other departments within this region. A long-beaked bird is perched
atop the head. Lower San Jorge River region. Early Zenú Goldwork Group. Ca. A.D. 1-1000.
Tumbaga. 2⅞" h. x 4" w. Museo del Oro (32914)

ALCARRAZA: BOWL WITH HEAD

The hemispherical shape of the upper eyelid, in combination with the straight narrow lower lid, makes
the eyes appear to be closed. It is unclear whether the artist intended a full head in the round or
only a face emerging masklike from the body of the vessel. The clearly defined bowl suggests that a
head was intended while the restricted portrayal of head hair emphasizes the face, rather than
the head. Perhaps the ambiguity is intentional. Calima region. Ilama style. Ca. 1000 B.C.-A.D. 1.
Pottery with traces of red-brown slip. 8⅛" h. x 6⅝" w. Museo del Oro (CC4481)

112.

114.

ANTHROPOMORPHIC VESSEL

The artist has imparted a distinct personality to the vessel by means of a highly restrained use
of modeling and appliqué to depict facial features and legs. The vessel itself serves as the body. The
open mouth with filed teeth, in combination with the coffee-bean-shaped eyes, gives the figure the
appearance of constrained tension. Muisca region. Muisca style. Ca. A.D. 900-1600.
Grey-white pottery. 10¼" h. x 12⅜" w. Museo del Oro (CM-1183)

ANTHROPOMORPHIC POLE

113.

The body of the figure blends with the column. Legs are not indicated. The upper body is rendered in a
classic Muisca style typified by the long fillets of appliqué clay used for the arms and the elliptical fillets of
clay used to indicate the eyes and the mouth. The figure holds unidentified objects in each hand, and
a large oval pendant hangs from the neck. Muisca region. Muisca style. Ca. A.D. 900-1600. Buff pottery
with cream and white paint. 19⅜" h. x 3½" w. Museo del Oro (CM12900)

139.

survive long under tropical conditions. Because of the uncontrolled nature of the digging there, we have no complete house plans or undisturbed floors, but the cemetery has yielded pottery vessels modeled in the shapes of houses (fig. 6). These models do not show details of construction, but we can safely assume that these prehispanic houses had walls made of vertical poles (perhaps of bamboo) plastered with mud. The roofs, which were thatched with palm leaves, sloped to shed the rain, which can be heavy at certain times of year. Indeed, some houses may have stood on supports to reduce the risk of flooding. Finally, the decoration on pottery models suggests that facades may sometimes have been painted with geometric designs.

Excavations in the domestic area have produced quantities of household rubbish: broken pottery, ash and charcoal, carbonized maize cobs, animal bones, and residues from craft activities including goldworking (in the form of tiny beads, scraps of wire, and miniature zoomorphic pendants).

A series of offerings gives some insight into the household rituals of ordinary people. In the upper Malagana-period strata of the excavation were pottery jars in the form of kneeling women resting on their heels. Some were placed close to miniature pottery "tables," each one circular with four legs. These were often deposited in pits, apparently as offerings (fig. 7). The majority of the figure-jars contained rock-crystal beads placed where the legs join the body. Quartz and rock crystal were important materials for the people of Malagana, and immense quantities of stone beads have come from their tombs. In the domestic part of the site, beads of different shapes and sizes were deposited either singly or in groups inside little jars. They were also found in rectangular concentrations as if originally packed in baskets or boxes that have not survived. Other offerings included the bones of snakes, birds, peccaries, and dogs.

ALCARRAZA WITH LEGS

The incised decoration of the red-slipped attached foot-form vessels contrasts markedly with the simple bichromatic decoration of the central *alcarraza*. Since the original context of this vessel is unknown, it is impossible to say whether it was a companion to a second *alcarraza* with attached clenched fist vessels. The iconographic significance of the composition is unknown. Department of Valle del Cauca. Malagana style. Ca. 150 B.C.-A.D. 200. Pottery with variegated slip. 7⅜" h. x 9⅜" w. Private collection

115.

ALCARRAZA WITH ARMS

The negative resist decoration on both the central vessel and attached fist forms is also common to the Yotoco culture of the Calima region. The significance of this composition is difficult to determine. The clenched fist is a common icon in the art of the Moche culture (ca. 100 B.C.-A.D. 700) of the north coast of Peru but is unusual in Colombia. Department of Valle del Cauca. Malagana style. Ca. 150 B.C.-A.D. 200. Pottery with variegated slip. 7½" h. x 7½" w. Private collection

116.

Unless deposited for ritual purposes, complete or spectacular objects are not to be expected in domestic areas either today or in the past, and our knowledge of these things comes from tomb contents, supplemented by the personal accounts of those who took part in the events of 1992. Given the history of the discovery, we know more about death at Malagana than about everyday life there.

Hundreds of graves were destroyed, although the true number can never be known. The tombs consisted of rectangular shafts or pits—some shallow, others nine feet or more in depth. Occasionally the walls were reinforced with river stones or the floor paved with stone slabs. Typically, the bodies lay on their backs on the tomb floors, but a few corpses were in flexed positions. Some bodies had been burned; others were incomplete, represented only by the skull, long bones, or the ribs and vertebrae (Rodríguez et al. 1993). One burial was contained in a finely decorated urn (fig. 8).

fig. **8**

BURIAL URN WITH RED SLIP

and incised decoration from the Malagana cemetery. Museo del Oro (CMa 13004). Photo courtesy of Museo del Oro, Santafé de Bogotá.

An unusual tomb, found partially looted, contained one hundred twenty metates, the flat stones on which maize was ground into flour. On top of these the body had been laid. Two gold beads were recovered from the coarse sand adhering to the metates, and two vessels were found on the floor of the tomb (fig. 9). The rest of the contents, reportedly very rich, had already been removed by looters (Botiva and Forero 1994).

The funerary evidence makes very clear that Malagana society was stratified or ranked and that the ruling elite had access to large quantities of costly prestige goods (Herrera et al. 1994; Archila 1996). Most tombs were relatively poor, but the few elite tombs were filled with the exquisite gold objects that have made Malagana famous. Other items were imported from distant regions. Such exotic items, along with esoteric knowledge, were sources of economic, political, and supernatural power in societies of chiefdom type. The finest items from the tombs carry symbolic designs that refer to the cosmology, rituals, and belief systems of the Malagana people.

One of the richer tombs at the site was a rectangular shaft about ten feet deep. Its floor was paved with some twenty squarish blocks of white granitic stone. Other stones of the same material covered the sides of the pit, while more than fifty slabs of different sizes were placed over the body. Sufficient traces of the skeleton remained to show that the corpse had been laid on its back with the head towards the south. Three sheet gold masks, one on top of the other, covered the head. In the neck area were several strands of beads made of various materials: little tubes of sheet gold, miniature stylized birds cast from solid gold, several kinds of greenstone beads (some also in the form of birds), globular beads of purplish, bluish, and black stones, and enough small stone beads to make up a string some fifty yards long. There were also beads made of red-lipped *Spondylus* shell imported from the Pacific Coast.

The chest of the corpse was covered with a row of gold pendants shaped like stylized bats, and over the lower part of the body was a group of bone tubes (or perforated beads) that may have been attached to a skirt or loincloth. A line of quartz beads separated the legs, and a sheet gold mask covered the feet. A niche in the wall of the shaft above the head of the skeleton held two pots: one a double-spouted vessel with a bridge handle, locally known as an *alcarraza*, with a globular body surmounted by the figure of a woman lying on her back; the other a bowl supported on four little feet. Both shapes are characteristic of the Ilama period.

Rich tombs like this one show that the chiefs and nobles of Malagana were interred fully dressed in all their finery. In addition, observers present at the initial discovery report that extra items were piled up in the corners of the burial pits. Stains in the surface patina of certain sheet gold objects corroborate this habit of stack-ing valuable objects one on top of another, whether on the corpse itself or on the floor of the tomb. Breastplates and chest ornaments, in particular, still retain the marks of multiple rows of gold beads on the back, as if the body had been covered in layer upon layer of jewelry (fig. 10). These splendid gold items and the stone necklaces, large and showy but also heavy and awkward, were not for everyday wear. Instead, they were the ceremonial attire of chiefs and members of the elite families. The finest gold artifacts, no matter how beautiful, were never merely decorative, but also functioned as political and religious status symbols, items of regalia, and indicators of high office.

In contrast to the rich interments of the elite, ordinary people were buried with only a few simple items, such as one or two pots and a few beads or shells. Some of the poorest tombs contained no burial offerings at all.

Burial No. 4 within the area of controlled excavation has a radiocarbon date of 90 B.C. ± 60 years, and belongs to the poorer category of tomb. The body, found about one foot below the present ground surface, was extended on its

fig. 9
TWO VESSELS,
*left behind by treasure hunters,
from the "tomb of the
metates" at Malagana.*

back with the head facing northeast. The skull had been intentionally deformed by binding in infancy (a frequent cosmetic practice in the New World), while the bone was still soft and malleable. The teeth were worn, and some were broken (Gonzalo Correal, personal communication). The head and shoulders rested on a layer of greenish silty clay, and two plain bowls had been placed near the right shoulder.

Another tomb, Burial No. 7, was found about five feet below the surface and had several curious features. The skeleton of a young man lay extended on its back, head to the northeast, but his jaw had been removed, presumably at the time of burial, and replaced by an unusually large, robust mandible that clearly belonged to someone else. At each side of this jaw was a rounded quartz bead (fig. 11), apparently placed in the cheek cavity when the man was buried. The tomb also contained a double-spouted *alcarraza* with a stylized bird on top of the globular body—a form that marks the transitional stage between the Ilama and Yotoco periods in the Calima region. This tomb had a radiocarbon date of 140 B.C. ± 60 years.

In spite of the huge quantity of artifacts from the tombs at Malagana, our knowledge of the cultural repertoire remains far from complete. Because all perishable items have rotted away, we have lost the cotton clothing, feather head-dresses, baskets, wooden tools, and foodstuffs that must have been buried with the dead for the journey to the afterworld.

fig. 10

DETAIL OF THE REVERSE SIDE
of a breast ornament from the
Malagana cemetery, showing
the impressions of
multiple bead necklaces.

Somewhere around 1000 B.C. the inhabitants of the Calima region in the Western Cordillera began to make pottery in a distinctive local style. Since we have no idea what language these people spoke or what they called themselves, archaeologists have named this culture Ilama after a district in the Calima region. Few Ilama settlements have been excavated, but a number of pottery vessels are modeled to represent a group of small rectangular houses arranged round a larger central building (cat. no. 118). Although best known for their pottery, the Ilama were competent goldsmiths and also carved small figures and other items from a green stone found locally. Their potters were highly skilled, and those who made the characteristic fine-incised and modeled wares may well have been specialists. A limited number of shapes—bowls, beakers, and, particularly, double-spouted *alcarrazas* with bridge handles—were used to model a wide range of animal, human, and mythical figures. Details were emphasized with incision and with black or occasionally white paint on a dark red or chestnut ground.

Birds such as owls or doves are often represented in Ilama pottery, as are stylized, probably feline quadrupeds with curly tails. Human figures include naturalistic representations

HEAD AND FEET ELEMENTS

Despite their diminutive size, each element is clearly formed and detailed, which is characteristic of late Tairona brownware. The purpose of these figurines is unknown. The use of more than one material in the manufacture of a figurine is extremely rare in Colombia. Such composite figures are known for the Malagana complex of the Cauca Valley, where body parts in gold and some other unidentified material that has decomposed are known. Composite gold and bone figures are also found in Panama. Tairona region. Late Tairona style. Ca. A.D. 1000-1600. Grey-brown pottery. (A) 1⅛" h. x ⅞" w.; (B) ⅞" h. x ⅞" w.; (C) 2" h. x 1" w.; (D) 1⅜" h. x 1¼" w.; (E) 1⅜" h.; (F) ⅝" h. Museo del Oro (CT9637,39,41,42,43,44)

117.

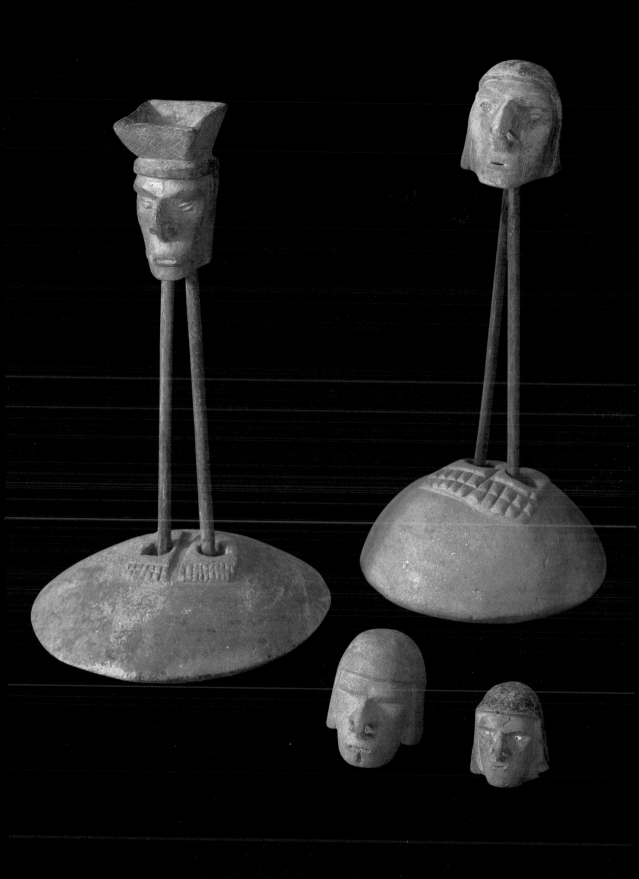

of men and women, some with swollen throats as if suffering from goiter. Recent studies have shown that this complaint can be caused by substances present in some of the local rocks near the springs that provided drinking water. Particularly well known in Ilama ceramics are the *canasteros* or "basket-bearers." Almost always male, they invariably carry a large basket-shaped receptacle. In some examples the basketry structure is clearly represented.

Also found on Ilama-period pottery are creatures belonging to a category in which elements characteristic of several different animals are fused and combined, while such features as hair, limbs, or tail are often replaced by snakes. This composite category ranges from quadrupeds to a series of shapes in which the human element becomes increasingly dominant, eventually merging into the *canastero* form. Known to some archaeologists as the "Fabulous Beast" (Cardale Schrimpff 1989), this creature may represent a mythical being or ancestor figure that can appear in both animal and human form—a concept widespread in Amerindian myths and cosmology. Regional variants of this figure and its component elements of feline, bat, snake, tortoise, crocodile, and human were represented in gold, pottery, and other mediums in several cultures of South-western Colombia at this time, from San Agustín in the highlands to Tumaco on the coast.

fig. II
BURIAL NO. 7
from the excavations at Malagana, showing the muddy, waterlogged nature of the site. The quartz beads at either side of the jaw were probably placed in the cheeks of the corpse.

The origins of the Ilama style are still unclear. Various authors (e.g., Reichel-Dolmatoff 1965, 85, 114) have suggested influence or even migration from the Pacific Coast to the interior, but the presence in the deepest strata of the Malagana excavation of pottery that, on stylistic grounds, may be ancestral to Ilama, reopens the entire debate. Unfortunately, as

ALCARRAZA: VILLAGE SCENE

118.
The central house may represent the ceremonial house of the village. Incised lines are used to indicate pathways. The curious arrangement of the houses suggests a possible cosmological model. Four larger paths mark off the four directions. The connected paths to the smaller houses form an elliptic, similar to the pathway of the sun as it moves from east to south, to west, to north. The larger paths may mark the rising and setting suns while the smaller houses may mark the solstice sunrises and sunsets. Calima region. Ilama style. Ca. 1000 B.C.-A.D. 1. Pottery with light brown slip. 8⅜" h. x 6¾" w. Museo del Oro (CC5620). Publications: Bray 1978, no. 550; Cardale de Schrimpff et al. 1991, no. 22.

ALCARRAZA: HOUSE MODEL

119.
This elegant *alcarraza* comprises three formal levels: a base of four globular chambers, a rooflike structure, and a handle with two spouts. Each solid red chamber alternates with a resist-decorated white chamber. Among groups in South America who still use the ancient gender-based dualism, when red is contrasted with white, red represents the female element and white the male element. When so contrasted, fertility is usually implied. Department of Valle del Cauca. Malagana style. Ca. 150 B.C.-A.D. 200. Pottery with red and white slip and resist decoration. 8⅞" h. x 7" w. Private collection. Publications: Archila 1996, pl. 33.

we have explained, the age of this Proto-Ilama pottery is ambiguous, and for the moment the question of Ilama origins is unanswerable.

At about the time of Christ the unity of the Ilama world began to break up, with the Calima and Cauca Valley regions following separate artistic paths. In Calima this is the Yotoco period, and in the Cauca Valley we can talk of a distinctive Malagana style. In Malagana-period tombs the finest pots are jars and double-spouted *alcarrazas*, modeled in the shapes of human figures, animals, birds, turtles, bats, and fantastic personages who may be deities or mythological figures. While shapes and motifs are shared with all of the neighboring areas, the potters of the Malagana period had technical and aesthetic preferences that make their wares instantly recognizable.

All the pottery was shaped by hand without the aid of a wheel or mold. The clay, fired to a café-au-lait color, was used as a decorative element in its own right, as can be seen in the contrast between the painted areas and the untreated spouts and handles on several items in this publication. Armbands were also left unpainted. Normally, though, most of the vessel surface was covered with a red paint or slip, sometimes in combination with zones of white. Further decoration was carried out by means of incision or resist painting, also called negative painting, a technique that was widespread in northern South America. The vessel was first slipped or painted in white and/or red; designs were then painted in a "resist" material like wax, liquid clay, or some resinous substance; finally, the pot was either dipped into an organic liquid or smudged with black smoke. The black stain was absorbed by the unprotected surfaces, but those parts covered with the resist material revealed their original color once this protection was removed. The overall effect is one of high contrast, with complex but rather fugitive fine-line patterns over a red or white background.

fig. 12

ILAMA-PERIOD NECKLACE

of hammered and embossed sheet gold beads. Each has the form of a female figure whose lower body is in the shape of an unidentified animal. Found in, or near, Restrepo (Calima region). The same concept can be seen on the lime flask in figure 13. Museo del Oro, Santafé de Bogotá (29270)

The negative painted designs of the Malagana period are carefully executed. One of the most common motifs, effectively a trademark for the Malagana style, is a crisscross or net-like arrangement with little dots or crosses inside the squares of the lattice. Some of the decorative motifs on the pottery also appear incised or embossed on the goldwork, thus serving to link the two mediums. The crisscross design is one of these; another is the "square spiral" design found on the armbands of figurative *alcarrazas* and on a pair of sheet gold trumpets (Archila 1996, pl. 76).

The modeled pottery and gold figures give some idea of how the people of the Malagana period looked. Both men and women are usually represented nude, with the genital areas exposed, but sometimes the sex of the figure is not indicated at all, leaving gender ambiguous. This lack of clothing may be an artistic convention rather than a picture of real life, for some of the miniature figurines made in gold have loincloths as well as leg ornaments. One of the most reliable clues to gender is hairstyle. Women wear their hair long, hanging down below the shoulders, while the men wear theirs cropped short. These hairstyle conventions are followed both in pottery and on a series of gold pendants, staff finials, and lime flasks in the shape of human beings.

Embossed designs on gold masks, like the painted designs on the faces of human-figure *alcarrazas*, perhaps indicate tattooing, scarification, or face paint. The number of ceramic figures classifiable as male or female is too small for us to be able to draw statistical conclusions, but certain trends can be tentatively identified. In pottery, though not in gold, women are most commonly represented in a kneeling position, resting on their heels, although some are in the more active poses that sometimes characterize the Malagana style. Men, in contrast, sit or squat on the ground in a variant of the Ilama "canastero position" (cat. no. 20) or with their arms folded across their knees (cat. no. 19). A few males (but no women) are seated on the low stools that sometimes signify shamanic or chiefly status (cat. no. 1).

There are also hints of gender-specific jewelry and other accessories. Only males wear elaborate crowns, and one *alcarraza* in the form of a seated man has a wide, elaborate belt painted white and red (cat. no. 1). On the other hand, patterned armbands seem to have been worn only by women, some of whom have carrying bags suspended from a strap across the forehead. In one case the negative-painted designs on the bag seem to represent a complex variety of knotless netting, or "looping," a technique much used for the manufacture of bags by present-day Indian groups. The same attention to detail can be seen on the basket carried by a Malagana-period *canastero* in the exhibition (cat. no. 20). In this particularly realistic example, the structure (indicated by negative paint) shows the cross-in-lozenge design still used for basketry by the Cuna Indians of Northwest Colombia (Cardale de Schrimpff 1992b, fig. 136).

From approximately 500 B.C. to A.D. 500, the regional cultures of Southwest Colombia shared a common goldworking tradition distinct from that of the central and northern parts of the country (Pérez de Barradas 1954; Plazas and Falchetti 1983; Plazas and Falchetti 1985; Plazas and Falchetti 1986). This Southwestern Tradition links the archaeological

MASK

Ceramic masks in this style are very rare. The known masks all depict a heavily wrinkled face, indicating great age. It is tempting to see in these masks a depiction of the Calima equivalent of the Mesoamerican Lord of Fire, an aspect of the solar deity and avatar of the cosmic duality. In Mesoamerica the Lord of Fire is depicted with a wrinkled face and only two teeth, hinting at his dual nature. The two protuberances under and at each side of the mouth may be a Calima convention evoking symbolism similar to the two teeth of Mesoamerican iconography. Calima region. Ilama style. Ca. 1000 B.C.-A.D. 1. Light brown pottery. 7 ½" h. x 5 ¾" w. Private collection

MASK

The cultures of Highland Nariño are closely related to similar groups on the Ecuadorian side of the border, and it is sometimes impossible to distinguish the art of one from the other. Four figures holding bowls or jars adorn the top of the head. Below the figures is a headband decorated with a series of articulated chevrons, which symbolizes water among some groups. The four figures may be pouring water from their jars. If so, the mask may represent a rain deity. The four figures may be his assistants. Highland Nariño region, Department of Nariño. Tuza style. Ca. A.D. 1250-1500. Pottery with cream slip. 11 ¼" h. x 7" w. Private collection

MASK

120.

The mask is similar in style to masks depicted on the walls of underground burial vaults *(hypogea)* found in the Tierradentro region of Colombia. The significance of the mask is unknown. Tierradentro region. Style and date unknown. Pottery with traces of cream slip. 8 ⅛" h. x 7" w. Private collection zones of Tumaco, Calima, San Agustín, Tierradentro, Tolima, and Quimbaya. Within the Greater Southwest, each regional group had its own individual history and art style, but trade products demonstrate that goods readily circulated among all of the local chiefdoms. If art and iconography reflect belief systems, it seems likely that the links among the southwestern communities were intellectual and aesthetic, as well as technological.

In metallurgy the southwestern artisans preferred to work with relatively pure gold rather than the alloys more popular elsewhere. They were capable of fine quality casting by the lost-wax method, with a special liking for miniature three-dimensional human and animal figures, but their most spectacular products were large, hammered, and embossed sheet items made for ceremonial use. Over most of the Southwest, goldsmiths made the same categories of object—masks, crowns and diadems, necklaces and breastplates, earspools, nose ornaments, pendants, tweezer-shaped artifacts, lime flasks—but interpreted the basic themes in slightly different ways (Archila 1996). The same is true of pottery. One of the forms that links all of the southwestern cultures is the double-spouted *alcarraza*, sometimes made with a whistle in place of one of the spouts. Everywhere, too, there is modeled pottery, along with a range of decorative techniques incorporating colored slips and negative painting.

fig. **14**
SHEET GOLD DIADEM
from the same tomb as the lime flask (fig. 13) at Malagana. The general H-shaped form, and also the stylized human figure, can be matched at San Agustín. Museo del Oro, Santafé de Bogotá (33335)

In both pottery and metallurgy Malagana shares these characteristics but also represents a new local culture within the Southwestern Tradition. Since they were located at the center of the Greater Southwest, we might expect that the rulers of Malagana would maintain trade contacts with all of their neighbors. Archaeological evidence for such a thriving commercial network is abundant.

One set of trade routes led westward over the low passes through the Western Cordillera, probably controlled by the Yotoco people, then down the great rivers that drain through the coastal rain forest and eventually reach the Pacific. A branch of this network by way of the Rio Dagua became the colonial route from the city of Cali to the Bay of Buenavantura and is followed by today's road and railway. In Colombia this coastal region, the Pacific terminus of the east-west routes, constitutes the Tumaco archaeological zone. Across the frontier, in Ecuador, identical material is named after La Tolita, the principal archaeological site, or after Esmeraldas, the northernmost coastal province of the country.

The cemetery at Malagana yielded an imported Tumaco-Tolita lime flask (fig. 13) and a pair of little Tumaco gold figurines (Ortiz 1996, no. 267 bis.), as well as ornaments carved from Pacific Coast shell and even whole sea shells sheathed with gold foil. Some of these complete shells appear to have served as lime containers, and the lime itself may well have been made from burned shell. The raw material for the drilled emerald beads found at Malagana must also come from the Pacific slope of the Cordillera, probably from Ecuador rather than Colombia, although the fact that some beads copy the shapes of Malagana gold examples suggests that some of the carving was done in the Cauca Valley.

The strong and continuous contacts between Malagana and the Calima region have already been discussed; indeed, the people of Calima may well have been the middlemen who transmitted items from the Pacific Coast to the interior valleys. Some support for this view is provided by the network of wide roads, in use during the Ilama and Yotoco periods, that converge on the Calima Valley. One of these roads links the Cordillera with the Cauca Valley some distance north of Malagana. Others, still unexplored, lead into the forests of the western slope of the Cordillera and probably connect with the system of navigable rivers in the Pacific lowlands (Cardale de Schrimpff 1996).

A second trade route followed the river Cauca south-ward and upstream into the mountain massif that is also the origin of the Rio Magdalena. In this general area, where the headwaters of Colombia's great inter-Andean rivers almost meet, are the well-known archaeological sites of San Agustín (a complex of burial mounds and stone statues) and Tierradentro, famous for its underground painted tombs.

fig. 15

PLAIN, RED-SLIPPED BOTTLE
*in Ecuadorian Chorrera style
from the cemetery at
Malagana. Private collection*

Links between these two localities and Malagana were particularly close. Ilama pottery has been found in the Tierradentro region (Gnecco and Martínez 1995), and the Malagana cemetery has yielded several vessels in San Agustín and Tierradentro styles. The list of similarities includes plain red *alcarrazas*, red and white *alcarrazas* in the shape of human heads, and—most diagnostic of all—a series of monochrome, highly burnished, double-spouted pots with high loop-handles. Some of the domestic sherds from Malagana also bear a close resemblance to San Agustín fragments. In the reverse direction, a Malagana whistling jar identical to figure 3 was found in a tomb at Rio Chiquito, near Tierradentro, along with two vessels of local manufacture (Duque Gomez 1979).

Much of the early goldwork at San Agustín and Tierradentro can be precisely matched in material from the Malagana cemetery. Tierradentro, for example, has sheet gold masks with embossed decoration, H-shaped diadems, embossed bracelets (or perhaps earspools) with designs of fantastic creatures, and Tolima-style pendants in the form of human figures with outstretched limbs bent at the elbows and knees (Duque Gomez 1979; Bray 1978, nos. 458-65). The San Agustín area has a gold mask (Plazas and Falchetti 1986, fig. 46), a Pacific Coast shell sheathed in gold, miniature falcon-shaped beads, and a series of

153.

nose pieces, bracelets, Tolima figures, earspools, and diadems (fig. 14) identical to those of Malagana (Bray 1978, nos. 453-54; and collections of the Museo del Oro). The total number of gold pieces from Tierradentro and San Agustín is not large. Nevertheless, the similarities with Malagana are so precise that we must question whether these two sites had gold styles of their own or actually produced gold items in Malagana style.

From the mountains of Nariño on the Ecuadorian frontier the people of Malagana obtained a pair of gold ear discs embossed with faces (Archila 1996, pl. 51). Black obsidian, a natural volcanic glass, also came from the south and was used for occasional tools and for the manufacture of round mirrors. One mirror found in a tomb in the Malagana cemetery has a streak of gold and may have been used as a touchstone to test the purity of gold. The farthest traveled object of all is perhaps the ceramic bottle in Ecuadorian Chorrera style (fig. 15). Although several scholars have discerned Chorrera influence on the art of Calima and Malagana, this is the first direct Chorrera import to be identified.

In short, the detailed evidence now available allows us to place Malagana within the context of Colombian prehistory as a whole. It was the capital of a rich, powerful, and economically successful regional chiefdom that maintained trade links with all of its neighbors and was also the home of sophisticated potters and goldsmiths who shared in the artistic canons of the Southwestern Tradition.

NOTES

1 The excavations at Malagana were directed by Marianne Cardale Schrimpff, Leonor Herrera, and Carlos Armando Rodríguez.

2 The dates cited in the text are given in "radiocarbon" years, which due to a number of factors including variations over the centuries in the amount of carbon available in the atmosphere, do not always coincide with calendar years. The two dates that have been obtained for the Proto-Ilama occupation (405 B.C.-A.D. 75 and 393 B.C.-193 B.C.) are surprisingly late, both from the point of view of the stylistic differences between their pottery and the "classic" Ilama ware and also from the depth of sediments separating the two occupations.

MASK

Tuza-style masks, which are relatively rare, are generally full-sized face masks such as this. The half-closed eyes and partially downturned mouth impart a sense of inner contemplation. The bulge in the left cheek represents a wad of coca leaf. In prehispanic Colombia the chewing of coca was associated with ritual, contemplation, and the sacred. Highland Nariño region, Department of Nariño. Tuza style. ca. A.D. 1250-1500. Pottery with cream-colored slip. 7½" h. x 5½" w. Private collection. Publications: Labbé 1986, pl. 48; Labbé 1988, pl. 48

123.

MASK (FOLLOWING PAGES)

The mouth is slightly downturned indicating concern, and the eyes are sharply turned to one side gazing apprehensively. Pacific Coastal region, Department of Nariño. Tumaco-La Tolita style. 300 B.C.-A.D. 300. Grey-white pottery. 5⅝" h. x 7½" w. Museo del Oro (Ctu-5684)

124.

MASK

PECTORAL WITH MASKED HEAD

This pectoral is fashioned from embossed sheet gold. Other components, also of sheet metal, have been attached to the heart-shaped primary section by means of metal strips. The pectoral is cleft above the head of the central figure in the form of two bands, one on the right, one on the left. The two bands, however, are actually one unified band decorated with panels of stylized bird heads arranged complementarily. The central figure wears a large nose ornament that covers most of the face, in effect a mask that has both feline and bat-like characteristics. The iconography suggests that the central figure may be the solar deity. The feline-bat maskette may be an allusion to his night and underworld aspect. Most indigenous groups in the Americas believed that the phenomenal cosmos was composed of a dual-natured essence, which expressed itself in male and female, positive and negative aspects. The interaction of male and female principles was viewed as a dynamic relationship that resulted in the creation of new forms. The solar deity was the source of this essence in the world. The band of dots along the base of the band also suggests fertility as dots are used by indigenous groups to represent seeds, the source of new life. Calima region. Yotoco style. Ca. A.D. 1-800. Gold. 10" h. x 12" w. Museo del Oro (5370). Publications: Bray 1978, cat. no. 31e.

MASK

125. Masks in this style are rare. For comparative purposes see Reichel-Dolmatoff 1986, p. 70, fig. 38.
      Lower Magdalena River region. Malambo style. Ca. 1100-100 B.C. Mottled grey pottery. 4" h. x 4¾" w.
      Private collection

MASK

126. Ceramic face masks depicting an aged individual constitute a genre within the Ilama ceramic style.
      Calima region. Ilama style. Ca. 1000 B.C.-A.D. 1. Pottery with brown slip. 4⅞" h. x 4⅝" w. Private collection

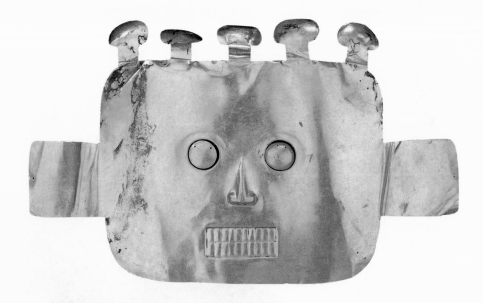

128.

This mask is fashioned from hammered sheet gold. The eyes are moveable. The bared teeth, effected with repoussé, are also found in Malagana clay art. A number of Malagana masks with moveable eyes have been recovered from funerary contexts. Cauca Valley region, Department of Valle del Cauca. Late llama or Malagana style. Ca. 200 B.C.-A.D. 200. Gold. 12½" h. x 20⅞" w. Museo del Oro (33402)

MASK

This mask is fashioned from embossed sheet gold. Details such as eyes and mouth are effected with repoussé. Masks such as this are found in funerary contexts. Calima region. Late llama style. Ca. 300 B.C.-A.D. 1. Hammered sheet gold. 8⅜" h. x 8⅞" w. Museo del Oro (3308)

129.

MASK

The llama metalsmiths used cut sheet gold in making masks. Usually these are decorated with repoussé. While it is possible that gold face masks were simply generic masks placed over the face of the dead, they may also represent the face of the solar deity. In other Colombian cultures gold was associated with the sun and the fertilizing energy of the sun. Calima region. Late llama style. Ca. 300 B.C.-A.D. 1. Gold. 6¹⁵⁄₁₆" h. x 8⅝" w. Dallas Museum of Art, The Nora and John Wise Collection; gift of Mr. and Mrs. Jake L. Hamon, the Eugene McDermott Family, Mr. and Mrs. Algur H. Meadows Foundation, and Mr and Mrs. John D. Murchison (1976.W.320)

130.

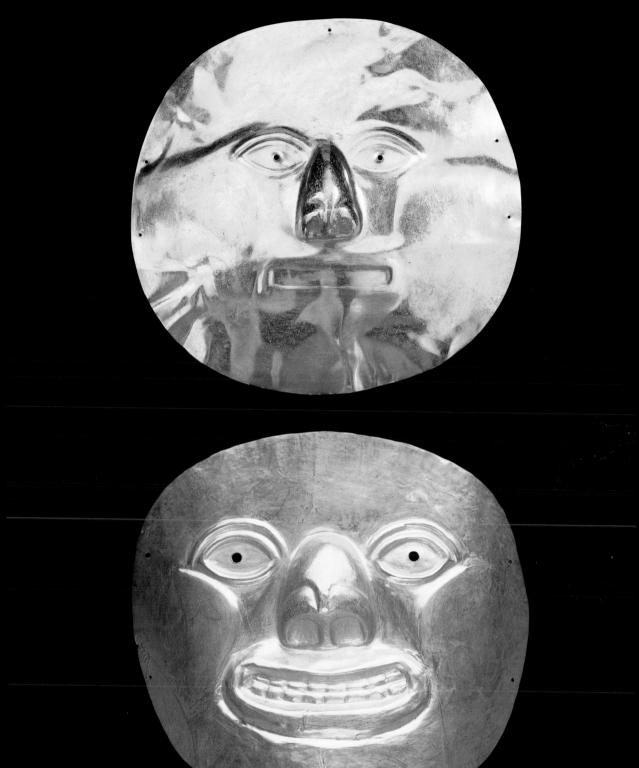

ZENÚ CERAMICS

FROM THE CARIBBEAN LOWLANDS

OF COLOMBIA

by Ana María Falchetti

PREHISPANIC

ceramics from the Caribbean Lowlands of northern Colombia reflect the presence in different regions and during different epochs of the diverse human groups that characterized the dynamic life of this important cultural region. Since the first pots were produced in the Caribbean Lowlands more than five thousand years ago, ceramics, being materials of special durability, have remained as traces of the many communities that developed pottery assemblages with distinctive characteristics. Just as these ceramic groups allow the archaeologist to distinguish among different societies, they also reveal information about the cultures from which they come.

Much can be learned from the ceramics of the Zenúes, the ancient inhabitants of the plains of the Colombian Caribbean Lowlands. To explore their social and ceremonial

ZOOMORPHIC JAR WITH TWO HEADS

131.

Janus-style figures, which share a single body, are relatively common in the art of pre-Columbian Colombia, particularly in the Ilama style of the Calima region and the Tairona style of northern coastal Colombia. Calima region. Ilama style. Ca.1000 B.C.-A.D. 1. Pottery with light brown slip. 8⅜" h. x 7⅞" w. Museo del Oro (CC4518)

132.

BOWL WITH RUNNING FELINES

In many respects the Malamboid style appears to have been the source of several artistic characteristics of later Tairona ware: the use of animal figures with two heads, a predilection for compositions with bilateral motifs, and the use of incising as a primary decorative technique. The dominant iconography here consists of paired and joined running felines seen in profile straddling the rim of the vessel. The other side of each feline is seen on the underside of the vessel. Tairona region. Malamboid style. Ca. 1000-100 B.C. Brown pottery with traces of white pigment. 3⅞" h. x 9⅜" w. x 11⅜" l. Private collection

BOWL WITH FELINES

The body of each feline is rendered in relief with incised details. The head of each figure, however, is modeled in the round and extends beyond the rim of the vessel. The feline, particularly the jaguar, was an important shamanic icon in northern Colombia. Tairona region. Malamboid style. Ca. 1000-100 B.C. Mottled brown pottery. 4¾" h. x 12⅞" w. Private collection

133.

ZOOMORPHIC VESSEL WITH TWO HEADS

Vessels such as this are characterized by an upward sweeping hollow body terminating at each end in the form of an animal or animal head. There is usually a large spout at the center of the vessel. Serpents, dragons, and crocodilians are closely associated with shamanism and concepts pertaining to the life force and shamanic powers such as shape-shifting and transformation. Tairona region. Late Tairona style. Ca. A.D. 1000-1600. Black pottery. 8⅞" h. x 13" w. x 6⅞" d. Instituto Colombiano de Antropología (COLCULTURA) (MN-A-86-VII2752)

134.

137.

ZOOMORPHIC BOWL WITH TWO HEADS

The iconography is more complex and sophisticated than it first appears. The vessel itself forms the body of a saurian or crocodilian with two heads. Adjacent and flanking each saurian head along the rim of the vessel are profile saurian heads, which also serve as the feet of the central figure. Secondary zoomorphic icons with serpentine elements are positioned at opposing ends of the midsection of the bowl. The primary heads and the secondary zoomorphic effigies at midpoint mark the four cardinal directions. Hypothetically, the larger fuller head marks off the east, place of the rising sun, the smaller, flatter head the west, i.e., the waning, setting sun. The profile heads would represent the rising and setting points of the winter and summer solstices, respectively, while the secondary zoomorphic icons would mark off the south and the north. The elliptical pattern outlined by the rim parallels the elliptical pattern traced by the daily movement of the sun. Tairona region. Malamboid style. Ca. 1000-100 B.C. Mottled brown pottery. 5⅜" h. x 13⅞" l. Private collection

138.

NOSE RING

The nose rings depicted on ceramic figures are modeled after pieces such as this, which were actually worn. Middle Magdalena River region. Tolima style. A.D. 200-1000. Gold. 1⅞" h. x 2⅛" w. Museo del Oro (33333)

ALCARRAZA: ZOOMORPH WITH TWO HEADS

135. The *alcarraza* form is clearly derived from cultures to the south, more specifically those from the Calima or Valle del Cauca regions. The dualism in this composition is given added emphasis by color coding areas of the vessel in red or white. The ethnographic literature indicates that when red is contrasted with white, red is associated with female qualities, white with male characteristics (see Labbé 1995, 89-104). Middle Cauca region. Style and date unknown. Pottery with red and white slip. 5½" h. x 9½" d. The Field Museum, Chicago (65124)

ZOOMORPHIC VESSEL

136. The sculptural and decorative characteristics of this composition are reminiscent of later Tairona incised brownware. Common to the Malamboid and Tairona incised brownware traditions are motifs depicting two crocodilian, feline, or other animal forms facing opposite directions, but sharing a common body. Both traditions used incising as a primary decorative technique. The lower body of the vessel is in the form of a large double-headed mythic creature with large serrated teeth. The arms or legs of the creature are in the form of serpent-bodied creatures. Along the rim are bird heads. The beak of each bird appears to be penetrating the head of the mythic creature, a theme also found in the pre-Columbian art of Costa Rica. Tairona region. Malamboid style. Ca. 1000-100 B.C. Pottery with brown and white paint/pigment. 14¼" l. x 7½" h. Private collection life, we have archaeological and ethnohistorical data, as well as the remnants of a Zenú tradition—most certainly mixed with other influences—among the present inhabitants of the San Andrés de Sotavento reservation in the lower Sinú River and surrounding areas. We are also able to use some aspects of the myths of other indigenous societies that survived in the vicinity of the Caribbean Lowlands to develop explanations that relate to the meaning and function of these ceramics for the Zenúes.

THE CONTEXT OF ZENÚ CERAMICS

The artificial prehispanic constructions

of the Caribbean Lowlands (fig. 1) of Colombia comprise the largest hydraulic project in South America. Based on information collected over the past twelve years, it has been possible to reconstruct the history of the settlement of the region for over two thousand

fig. 1
ARTIFICIAL PREHISPANIC DRAINAGE
*systems in the Lower San Jorge
River area. Photo Clemencia Plazas
and Ana María Falchetti.*

years and to identify the different groups that inhabited the area (Plazas and Falchetti 1981; Plazas and Falchetti 1986; Plazas and Falchetti 1990; Plazas et al. 1988; Plazas et al. 1993).

In the Caribbean plains, the exploitation of natural resources in various microenvironments favored both the development of stable economic systems and the emergence of complex societies. The Zenú people and their predecessors gradually occupied and explored these seasonally flooded plains, which were well known for their fertile soil and rich fauna (Plazas and Falchetti 1990). Sometime around the ninth century B.C., the settlers began building canals in the Lower San Jorge River (Plazas et al. 1993, 61). This hydraulic system would eventually cover a million acres in this area and 370 thousand acres along the lower course of the Sinú River (Plazas and Falchetti 1986).

Indigenous groups gradually fanned out along the Lower San Jorge River, and by the

ZOOMORPHIC VESSEL WITH TWO HEADS

The Naguanje style is as yet poorly documented. Pre-Columbian belief has it that every form comprises a life force that results from the blending of two life streams, one essentially male and the other female. The pre-Columbian perspective on duality is best expressed in the cosmologies of the Nahua-speaking peoples of Mesoamerica and the Tukanoan-speaking peoples of the Northwest Amazon of Colombia. This composition implies a union of these dual forces. Tairona region. Naguanje style. Ca. A.D. 500-800. Pottery with black on white slip. 7⅞" h. x 13⅜" w. Museo del Oro (CT-12505)

139.

LID: MYTHIC ANIMAL WITH TWO HEADS

The Ranchería style is as yet poorly defined. The depiction of two joined figures is widespread in the Malamboid, Naguanje, Tairona, and Ranchería styles. The creature portrayed here appears to be a Ranchería version of catalogue number 139, which is rendered in the Naguanje style. North Santander, Baja Guajira region. Ranchería style. 500 B.C.-A.D. 1000. Pottery with black paint on white slip. 7¾" h. x 10⅜" w. Museo del Oro (CS-12804)

140.

second century A.D. cultural changes had resulted from the evolution of local populations together with a possible foreign influence (Plazas et al. 1993, 127). Artificial platforms for housing, which were lined up in rows on the waterways, and funerary mounds (fig. 2) became more common, and a style of ceramics belonging to the Zenú modeled-and-painted tradition was gradually introduced and widely distributed throughout the San Jorge River basin and surrounding areas. Characterized by a distinctive cream-colored ware, complex shapes sculpted with modeled decoration, and geometric designs in red paint, the modeled-and-painted tradition included local ceramic groups united by their use of common materials, manufacturing techniques, and forms and decorations.

This ceramic tradition, together with Zenú goldwork (Falchetti 1995), is associated with a cultural complex belonging to communities that had different characteristics and geographical locations but were also closely related, shared funeral and settlement patterns, and enjoyed the same relationship to their natural environment.

fig. **2**

THE ZENÚ FUNERARY MOUNDS,
in which the dead were buried with rich offerings of gold and ceramics, are numerous in Colombia's Caribbean Lowlands. Photo Clemencia Plazas and Ana María Falchetti.

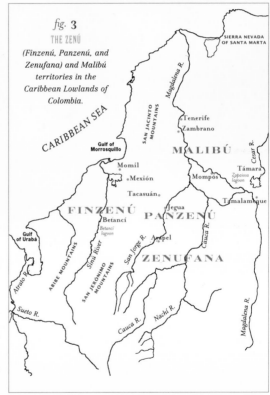

fig. **3**

THE ZENÚ

(Finzenú, Panzenú, and Zenufana) and Malibú territories in the Caribbean Lowlands of Colombia.

ZOOMORPHIC VESSEL

Vessels on four supports with a large central spout are a standard form within the Tairona ceramic repertoire. The form is employed as a "canvas" on which to portray a number of mythological or cosmological themes. A common variant incorporates a dragon head at each end of the vessel. In this example, a stylized animal head is at one end and a seated figure at the other. The seated figure represents either a priest impersonating a bat deity or the deity himself, as is indicated by the snout and headgear. Tairona region. Tairona style. Ca. A.D. 1000-1600. Black pottery. 10" h. x 12½" l. x 6½" w. The Bowers Museum of Cultural Art; gift of Susan Lancaster (95.38.1)

141.

fig. 4

FEMALE FIGURES

such as this one in the
granular-and-incised tradition
have been produced in
the San Jorge River basin and
surrounding areas since
the beginnings of the Christian era.
Museo del Oro,
Santafé de Bogotá (CS 12585).
Photo Rudolph.

fig. 5

THIS FEMALE FIGURE

in the modeled-and-painted
tradition is from the middle
reaches of the San Jorge River.
The figure is adorned with a
semilunar breastplate, a nose
ornament with extensions, and
semicircular ear ornaments
that may represent the
cast-filigree ornaments
characteristic of Zenú goldwork.
Museo del Oro,
Santafé de Bogotá (CS 12766).
Photo Rudolph.

These are the cultural manifestations that we can attribute to the Zenúes, whose highest achievements occurred between the fifth and tenth centuries in the area of the Lower San Jorge River (Plazas et al. 1988; Plazas et al. 1993). By the tenth century related communities occupied a large part of the San Jorge River, settling the middle reaches of the river, where they built important grave mound cemeteries (Plazas and Falchetti 1981; Plazas et al. 1993). They also occupied the intermediate area between the San Jorge and Sinú rivers and very possibly the Lower Cauca River to the east (Falchetti 1997a).

Similar processes took place around the Sinú basin with the development of the Betancí Complex (Reichel-Dolmatoff 1957), which was characterized by a distinctive material culture, including ceramics related to the modeled-and-painted tradition of the San Jorge River area, and by the construction of raised house platforms and funerary mounds. Cultural manifestations represented by the Betancí Complex are strongly associated with the Zenú populations found in the Sinú River area by the Spanish conquistadors in the sixteenth century (Reichel-Dolmatoff 1957; Plazas and Falchetti 1981).

After the tenth century, the Zenúes progressively left the floodplains of the Lower San Jorge River and the surrounding areas, allowing the entry of groups related to the Malibúes around the fourteenth century. Strong fluctuations in the flood levels may have been partly responsible for the breakup of this growing society, which had for centuries controlled the waters in the seasonally flooded plains (Plazas et al. 1993).

The Malibúes' traditional habitat was the lower eastern area of the Magdalena River (Plazas and Falchetti 1981). The Zenúes survived in the higher savannahs near the floodplains and also in the Sinú basin, where the Spanish conquistadors would find remains of ancient, more populous habitation. The Spanish were surprised by the complex social and political organization of the remaining Zenú settlements—a structure the Zenúes had managed to maintain despite the diminishment of their territories—and, in particular, by the extensive power of their *caciques*, or chieftains; and the influence of their ceremonial centers (Falchetti 1997a).

From the indigenous traditions recorded by Spanish chroniclers during the conquest and subsequent colonial period, together with archaeological data, we can deduce that there once existed a Greater Zenú, made up of three "provinces" (fig. 3) that were founded by three mythical rulers (Simón 1625/ 1981, vol. 5, 98). Panzenú, located in the San Jorge River basin, may have been especially dedicated to the production of foodstuffs through exploitation of the floodplains in agriculture and fishing. Although specialized artisans probably existed throughout the territory of Greater Zenú, a concentration of goldsmiths, potters, and weavers was reported to be in Finzenú, which was located in the Sinú River basin and environs (Plazas and Falchetti 1981). Finally, the chronicles place Zenufana on the Cauca and Nechí rivers and surroundings, a territory so rich in gold that its inhabitants dedicated themselves to mining. The Zenúes of the plains always maintained trading relations with these people.

fig. **6**

THIS SEMILUNAR BREASTPLATE
*with repoussé decoration is
hammered from high-content gold.
Pieces with this shape are common
among the ornaments represented
in the ceramic female figures
from the middle reaches of
the San Jorge River.
Museo del Oro, Santafé de Bogotá
(CS 25466). Photo Rudolph.*

fig. **7**

THE SHAPE OF THIS NOSE RING
*with lateral extensions is
distinctive of Zenú goldwork.
Museo del Oro, Santafé de Bogotá
(6477). Photo Rudolph.*

CERAMICS AND SOCIETY

The Zenúes were fundamentally lowland peoples.

In the sixteenth century they occupied the areas that correspond to the territories of Finzenú and Panzenú, where the Spanish found remnants of that hierarchical society whose cohesion was secured through intense ceremonial activity. Political power and religious power were closely joined: *caciques* and *mohanes* (priests or shamans) made up the governing group. The Zenú settlements of Finzenú on the Sinú River and Ayapel on the San Jorge River exercised their influence over these extensive regions (Castellanos 1601/1955, vol. 3, 78).

The main town of Finzenú was "the court of the Great Cacique or rather that of the Great Cacica and lady of many villages, her subjects, which she had in her province"

142.

INCENSE BURNER LID WITH MYTHIC ZOOMORPH

The artist has sculpted the winged figure around the central spout of the lid, but the head of the figure is cast from a mold. The figure blends human arms and legs with wings and the head of a fanged beast. The composition may represent a transformed shaman flying in his "soul body," or it may be a reference to a mythic beast from Tumaco mythology. Pacific Coastal region, Department of Nariño. Tumaco-La Tolita style. Ca. 300 B.C.-A.D. 300. Grey-white pottery. 6⅜" h. x 7" d. Private collection. Publications: Labbé 1986, no. 7; Labbé 1988, no. 7.

143.

BOWL WITH ATLANTEAN FIGURES

The bowl is supported by a series of anthropomorphic figures with legs splayed and arms outstretched. Neither the decoration nor the form of this vessel is typical of the Tairona style. Atlantean figures supporting bowls are more characteristic of ceramic ware found far to the south such as the Capulí Complex of Highland Nariño. The composition is probably a reference to Tairona myth or cosmology. Tairona region. Early Tairona style. Ca. A.D. 800-900. Pottery with light brown and dark brown slip. 7⅛" h. Museo del Oro (CT5615)

FIGURAL JAR WITH MYTHIC THEME

The composition—an anthropomorphic frog riding a large toad— is unique. The large sacklike parotid glands, atop and behind the eyes of the toad, are characteristic of the marine toad *Bufo marinus*, a species that secretes a highly toxic hallucinogenic milky secretion from its parotid gland and its skin. The frog's human characteristics suggest the figure is a transformed shaman, under the influence of a toad-skin generated hallucinogen. Calima region. Ilama style. Ca. 1000 B.C.-A.D. 1. Pottery with brown slip. 6⅜" h. x 5⅛" l. Private collection

144.

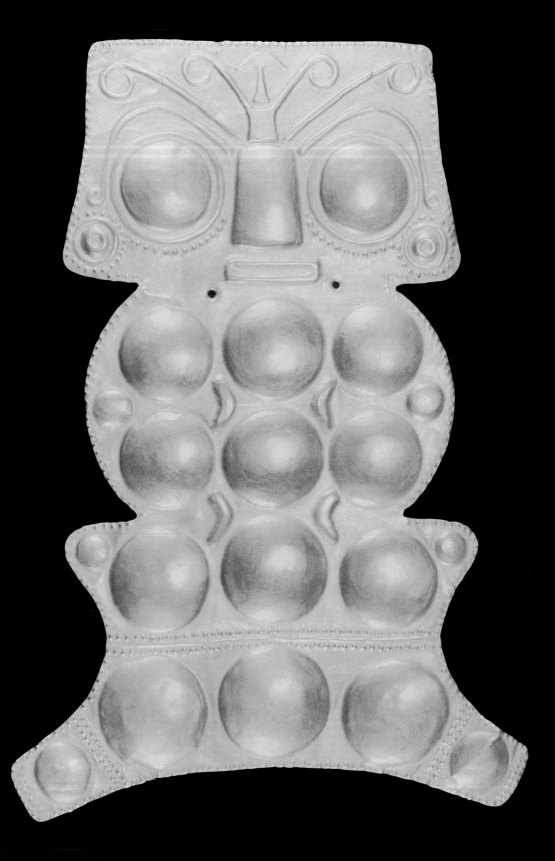

OWL PECTORAL

OCARINA: PRIEST IN ANIMAL GUISE

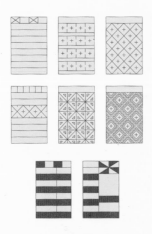

fig. **8**

SKIRT DESIGNS FOUND ON BETANCÍ CERAMIC FIGURINES
from the Sinú River region.
Drawing by Melba Rodríguez de León.

(Simón 1625/1981, vol. 5, 121). The Spanish were surprised by the great majesty and privileges of this *cacica*. The social and political importance of women was, however, integral to the indigenous tradition, as is reflected by the actions of the legendary *cacique* Zenufana, who decreed that his sister govern Finzenú (Simón 1625/1981, vol. 5, 98).

The numerous ceramic female representations produced in different areas over the centuries illustrate the importance of women in society and highlight the female principle in the ceremonial and funerary customs of many of the people who inhabited the Caribbean Lowlands in prehispanic times. Various figurines possibly produced during the first few centuries of the present era (cat. no. 85) reflect the cultural diversity of the ancient communities that populated the plains.

The figurines found in the Lower San Jorge River area represent an ancient tradition. Some of them, unadorned and made of a granular and durable clay produced before the beginning of the Christian era[1] (fig. 4), also appear to the east near the Lower Cauca and

OWL PECTORAL (PRECEEDING PAGES)

145. This pectoral is fashioned from embossed hammered sheet gold. The large repoussé discs used for the eyes of the owl are repeated over the surface of the figure and may represent the shaman's powerful vision. Owls are closely associated with shamanism and the powers of the night. Shamans are said to have penetrating vision that allows them to see into a patient's body to determine the cause of disease and to see events occurring far away. Among some groups they are believed able to impregnate a woman simply by projecting their fertilizing power through their eyes. The dots used as outline along the perimeter and under the eyes may be an allusion to fertility, as dots were used to symbolize seeds, potential points of new life. Lower Magdalena River region. Sinú style. Date unknown. Gold. 13⅝" h. x 9⅝" w. Museo del Oro (6371). Publications: Jones and Bray 1974, cat. no. 7.

OCARINA: PRIEST IN ANIMAL GUISE (PRECEEDING PAGES)

146. Finely detailed miniature figural whistles and *ocarinas* are typical artifacts of Tairona culture. They were most likely used by shamans and priests during rituals. Possibly a personage from Tairona myth or allegory, the figure appears to be an anthropomorphic feline in elaborate dress. In his left hand is a loop-handled vessel, an icon widely portrayed in pre-Columbian art from Mexico through Colombia. In the art of the Maya it is sometimes identified as holding incense. Tairona region. Late Tairona style. Ca. A.D. 1000-1600. Grey-brown pottery. 3⅜" h. x 2¼" w. Museo del Oro (Ct-12627)

PEDESTAL VESSEL WITH FIGURES

The figural art in this style is made up largely of jars in female form, kneeling female figures, and figures placed at opposite ends of a bowl or at the ends of strap handles found on jars or enclosed vessels. This example is exceptional in its composition, which depicts a ritual scene. Two anthropomorphic figures appear to be holding a platform atop of which is a feline. The animal stands on the lid. The handle forms a sheltering cavelike canopy above it. Middle San Jorge River region. Montelibano style. Ca. A.D. 800-1000. Buff pottery. 15" h. Museo del Oro (CS5979). Publications: Plazas et al. 1993, pl. 40A. **147.**

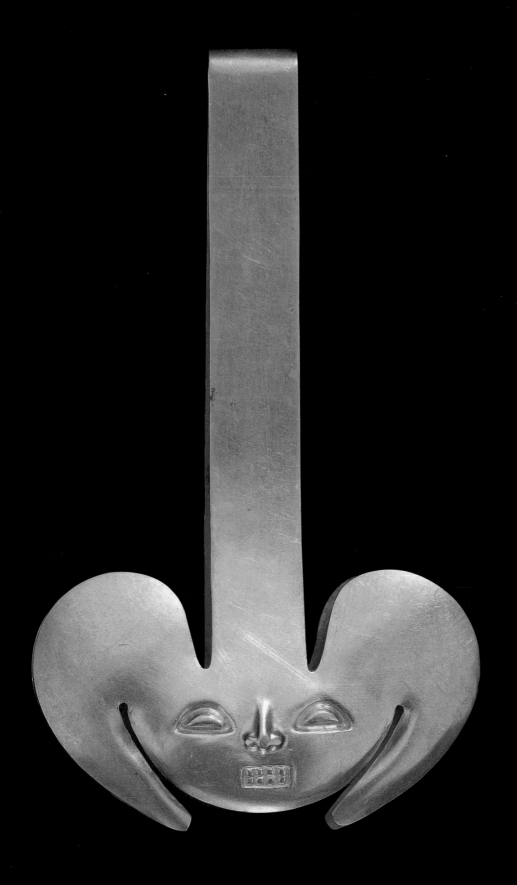

PINCERS IN THE FORM OF A CRAB

PEDESTAL BOWL WITH ARMADILLO

Lower Magdalena rivers (see Labbé 1988, pl. 24; Reichel-Dolmatoff 1986, fig. 65). These standing figurines wear no ornaments, but they do have orifices in their ears that might have served to suspend gold rings. The people who made the figurines built housing platforms along the waterways and lived in nucleated settlements, but there is still no evidence of funerary rites (Plazas et al. 1993). The female figures found in the funerary mounds of the Zenúes are distinctive and unmistakable. In structures built in the first ten centuries of our era, there are kneeling figurines adorned with diadems that belong to the modeled-and-painted tradition.[2]

fig. 9

THIS RITUAL CUP WITH COVER
in the modeled-and-painted tradition is from the San Jorge River region. Museo del Oro, Santafé de Bogotá (CS 4110). Photo Rudolph.

Numerous figurines that belong to a regional variation of the modeled-and-painted tradition (cat. no. 37; fig. 5; Sáenz Samper 1993) have been found in the middle course of the San Jorge River in tombs that are organized into cemeteries, including one dating from the tenth century. There are some male representations, but women, typically nude with exaggerated sexual areas (Sáenz Samper 1993), are predominant. Some figures are standing, but the majority are kneeling. A few are seated on benches to signal the social importance of the female—generally an attribute of *caciques* and shamans, the bench is a symbol of prestige and knowledge. These figurines are endowed with representations of ear ornaments, nose rings, and breastplates, ornaments that were originally produced in gold and accompanied the wearers to their tombs.[3] Differences in ornaments might signal differences in social rank: some have only a

PINCERS IN THE FORM OF A CRAB (PRECEEDING PAGES)

148.
The open mouth with bared teeth is a stock icon of the Malagana style. The facial details were effected with repoussé. The hemispherical eyes are also characteristic of Malagana gold and ceramic work. A human face has been superimposed on the body of a crab, suggesting that this is no ordinary crab but one of shamanic significance. Animal species were believed to have their own shamans. Alternatively, human shamans were said to be capable of transforming their "soul bodies" to assume the form of other animals. Department of Valle del Cauca. Late llama or Malagana style. Ca. 200 B.C.-A.D. 200. Gold. 4 ⅞" h. x 2 ⅞" w. Museo del Oro (33394)

PEDESTAL BOWL WITH ARMADILLO (PRECEEDING PAGES)

149.
Among a wide range of native American groups the armadillo is perceived as an essentially uterine symbol. The interlocking triangles used to decorate the body of the armadillo are emblematic of fertility. Middle Sinú River region. Betancí style. Ca. A.D. 1000-1500. Brown pottery. 25" h. x 11 ⅜" w. Museo del Oro (CS-12822)

BAT-SHAPED EAR ORNAMENTS

Ear ornaments in the form of stylized bats are characteristic of the Tolima region. The spiral ornaments are likely intended to represent eyes, here exaggerated to serve as metaphors for the shaman's penetrating vision. The bat is associated with the night, the night sun in its journey through the underworld, and the power of menstrual blood. Middle Magdalena River region. Tolima style. Ca. A.D. 200-1000. Gold. 2 ⅞" h. x 4 ¼" w.; 2 ¾" h. x 4 ⅛" w. Museo del Oro (5836 and 5837). Publications: Jones and Bray 1974, cat. nos. 98 and 99.

150.

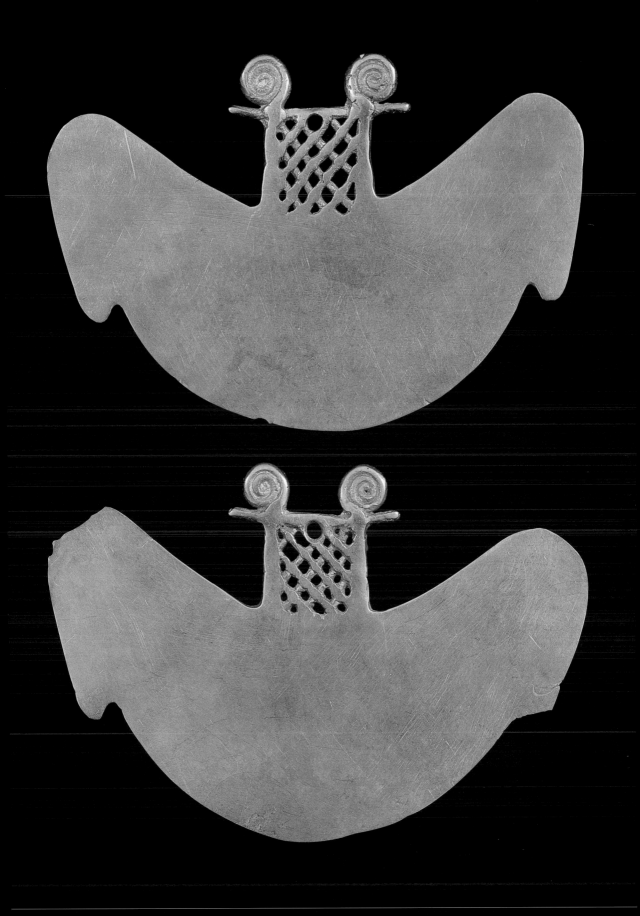

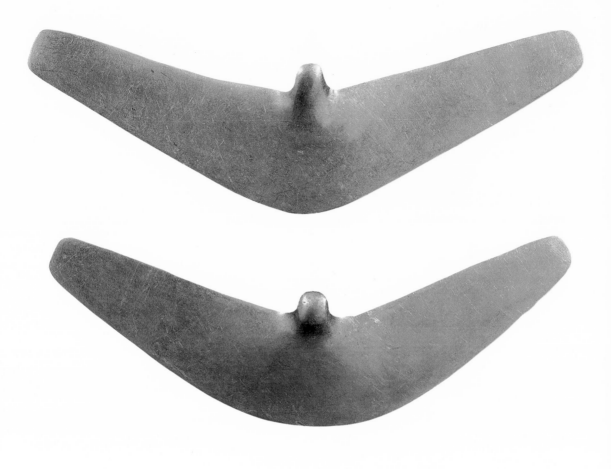

152.

BAT-SHAPED EAR ORNAMENTS

The simple contours of these ear ornaments suggest bats in flight. The bat is associated with the powers of the night, the night sun in its journey through the underworld, and menstrual blood. Department of Valle del Cauca. Late Ilama or Malagana style. Ca. 200 B.C.-A.D. 200. Gold. ⅜" h. x 5" w.; 1¼" h. x 4¾" w. Museo del Oro (33236, 33237)

GLOBULAR JAR WITH FELINE

151. The elegant and intricate incised decoration seen on this early vessel exemplify the precision of line, balance of form, and attention to detail characteristic of Tairona art. The predominant incised decoration consists of spirals and S-scrolls. The figure attached to the top of the vessel has a humanlike face, an animal body, and short elephantine legs, a blending of human and animal traits sometimes used to indicate the transformation of a human shaman into an animal form. It may also indicate that a mythic personage is intended. Tairona region. Early Tairona style. Ca. A.D. 600-800. Brown pottery. 7⅜" h. x 7⅛" w. Museo del Oro (CT5616). Publications: Oyuela-Caycedo 1986.

fig. 10

THIS MAN WITH MUSICAL INSTRUMENTS
and woman with receptacle
once decorated a Betancí vessel
from the middle reaches of the
Sinú River. Museo Sergio Restrepo S.J.,
Tierralta, Cordoba, Colombia.
Photo Ana María Falchetti.

fig. 11

THIS REPRESENTATION OF A JAGUAR
with anthropomorphic figures is in the
modeled-and-painted tradition.
Museo del Oro, Santafé de Bogotá
(12899). Photo Rudolph.

simple nose ring (cat. no. 38) while others have more numerous and elaborate adornments such as semilunar breastplates (fig. 6) or nose ornaments with extensions (fig. 7). Nevertheless, these figurines tend to be stereotyped and may therefore be the abstraction of a particular symbolism that governed both their meaning as a group and their mass production. The types of ornaments they carry are also homogenous; yet the nose rings in the form of an *n* (cat. no. 38) and nose ornaments in general may serve as a means for us to explore the possible meaning of certain ornamentation.

In the past, nose rings in the shape of an *n* were abundant in Zenú territory, in the lower Magdalena, and in neighboring zones. Sixteenth- and seventeenth-century sources record that nose rings were particularly prized among the Malibúes and that in the matrimonial exchange the groom was required to present one of these ornaments to his father-in-law. The Malibúes also played a crucial role in the trade of these and other metal pieces over large areas (Falchetti 1993; Falchetti 1995, 281-84, 289). A principal function of such exchanges was to achieve a balance in relations both within society and with other communities, in keeping with the norms that govern matrimonial alliances (Osborn 1995). This explains the importance of the objects exchanged, as well as their frequent identification with the female.

At present, ring-shaped nose ornaments are used by Cuna women in the northwest of Colombia and in Panama. According to their tradition, one of the culture heroes taught the Cuna how to make these ornaments (Vargas 1993, 107). The ceremony, during which the nose of a young woman is pierced to carry a gold nose ring, is very important (Herrera and Cardale 1974, 205), for this ornament recalls the role of the woman in the perpetuation of life and in the regulation of the marriage rules taught by the culture heroes (Morales 1997). These norms mark the differentiation between man and nature and affirm the identity of the social group. Similar concepts probably determined the recurrent use of certain gold

EAGLE PENDANT

The use of the braid pattern as trim along much of the perimeter of the figure is characteristic of Tairona goldwork. Pendants such as this are identical to those depicted hanging around the neck of figures portrayed in the ceramic art. The eyes are oversized and emphasize the power of vision. In Kogi iconography, the eagle is closely associated with the solar deity. Among many groups in Colombia, the solar deity is perceived as First Shaman, the source of all shamanic power. Tairona region. Late Tairona style. Ca. A.D. 1000-1600. Gold. 2⅜" h. x 2¼" w. Museo del Oro (13831). Publications: Bray 1978, cat. no. 300.

153.

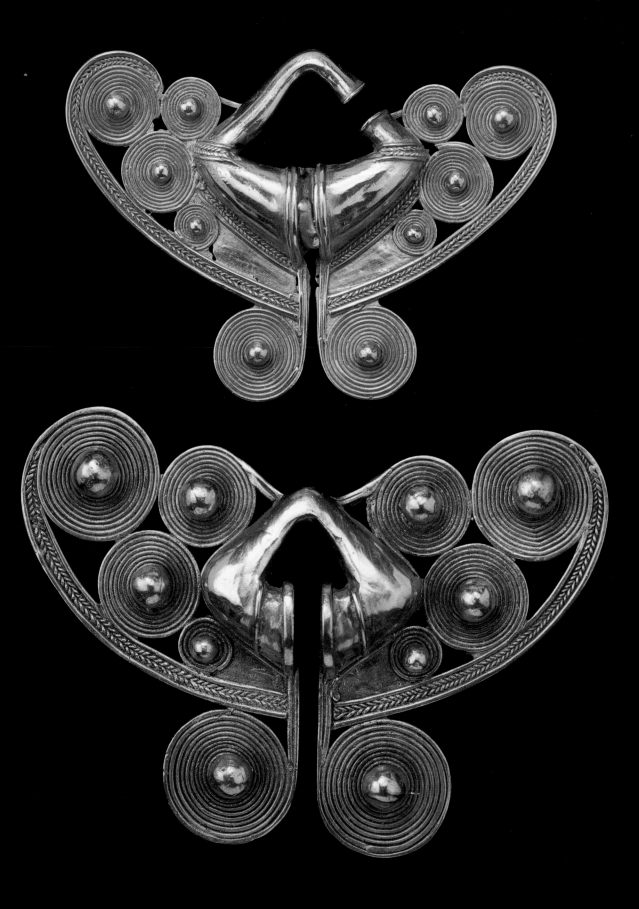

BOWL IN THE FORM OF A MONKEY

The color of the slip suggests the Tuza style rather than the earlier Capulí style. The monkey was a common motif in both styles although its use in Capulí is most often associated with small jars where monkey adornos are placed on the shoulder of the jar adjacent to the rim of the vessel. The monkey is also found as graphic decoration for pedestaled bowls and as modeled decoration placed at the ends of shell-shaped *ocarinas* modeled in clay. Among groups in South America the monkey is associated with the Monkey Constellation, which in turn is associated with the rainy season. It is unclear whether this association prevailed among the pre-Columbian peoples of Highland Nariño. Highland Nariño region, Department of Nariño. Tuza style. Ca. A.D. 1250-1500. Dark grey pottery. 2¼" h. x 7⅛" w. Museo del Oro (CN4602)

BUTTERFLY NOSE ORNAMENT

154. Cast using the lost-wax technique, the form is that of a stylized butterfly, a symbol of fertility and transformation among native groups in Colombia and elsewhere. The Kogi, who trace themselves to their Tairona forebears, refer to their priest-shamans as the guardians of fertility. Both the power to alter their shape and enhance fertility symbolically align shamans with butterflies. Tairona region. Late Tairona style. Ca. A.D. 1000-1600. Gold. 2⅜" h. x 3⅜" w. Museo del Oro (30443)

BUTTERFLY-SHAPED NOSE ORNAMENT

155. The form of this exceptionally large nose ornament—a butterfly or moth, replete with antennae—is specific to the Tairona. Tairona region. Late Tairona style. Ca. A.D. 1000-1600. Gold. 2⅞" h. x 4⅛" w. Museo del Oro (13428)

157.

ZOOMORPHIC JAR

Characteristically Tairona, the form of this vessel comprises five essential elements: a distinct base usually oval; a hollow elongated body; two "spouts," one of which is enclosed and shaped like the head of an animal; and a strap handle bridging the two spouts. The head is that of a bird with comb atop the head. Tairona region. Late Tairona style. Ca. A.D. 1000-1600. Black pottery. 9¾" h. x 9¾" l. Private collection. Publications: Labbé 1986, no. 156; Labbé 1988, no. 156.

158.

NECKLACE

The necklace is composed of thirty-six individual elements and in style and composition is very similar to another necklace, also in the Museo del Oro collection (20-289), which was found in the Rio Palomino region of Guajira, Magdalena. Each element is a stylized zoomorphic head, most likely representing a cayman. The cayman is associated in myth and ethnographic context with concepts of creative power and vitality. Tairona region. Late Tairona style. A.D. 1000-1600. Gold. 1⅜" h. x ⅝" w. Museo del Oro (29306)

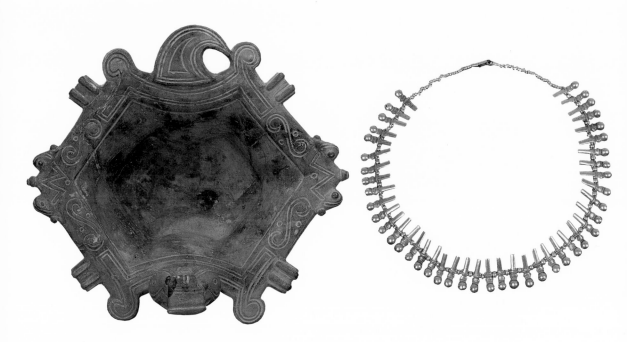

ZOOMORPHIC VESSEL

The Malamboid style appears to have indirectly contributed certain iconographic elements such as the cayman head to late Tairona art. The central image on the vessel is that of a cayman. The head and tail are clearly delineated, while the vessel itself forms the body of the animal. Frog heads are on each side of the vessel midpoint between the head and tail of the cayman. Four small panels mark off an X-pattern. The iconography appears to have astronomical significance. The cayman's head and tail and the two frog heads mark off the four cardinal directions. The upturned cayman head may represent the east and the rising sun; and the downturned tail, the west and the setting sun. The two frog heads mark the south and the north, respectively. The X-pattern delineated by the four flanges may indicate the winter and summer solstice rising and setting points. The basic cross and X-pattern marking the cardinal directions and solstice rising and setting points is found widely in the Americas. Tairona region. Malamboid style. Ca. 1100-100 B.C. Light brown pottery. 5¾" h. x 12½" w. Private collection. Publications: Labbé 1986, no. 159; Labbé 1988, no. 159.

160.

NECKLACE WITH BIRD-SHAPED BEADS

The necklace is composed of forty-three matched stylized bird-shaped beads. Birds were messengers and mediators between the forces of the earth and sky. Calima region. Style and date unknown. Gold. 19½" l. Private collection ornaments of specific shapes by Zenú women, pieces that appear in the tombs of the region and are represented in ceramic figurines.

The female figures in Betancí ceramics (cat. nos. 44, 49, 55) found in the Sinú River area are distinctive, sophisticated, and attractive. Their skirts are decorated with designs (fig. 8) reminiscent of the skirts worn by the Zenú women described in the Spanish chronicles. The writers thought that the differences in design "depended on the taste of each," but we now think that they may have identified family links or belonged to certain manufacturing centers, a tradition that has lasted through the centuries for certain items made in the region. The female Betancí ceramics are also represented with gold ornaments, namely earspools. While different from those on figurines found near the San Jorge River, these earspools are similar to those on the anthropomorphic figures of Zenú goldwork (cat. no. 111). Finally, ceramic Betancí figures have ornaments suspended from their necks that recall the gold pendants with multiple zoomorphic figures (cat. no. 30) that appear together with earspools (cat. no. 50) and other forms in the intermediate area between the Sinú and the San Jorge rivers and in Urabá[4] (Falchetti 1995, 120, 218). In this last region there exist ceramic female figures of a very local style that wear these ornaments (cat. nos. 18, 50) along with other figurines related to those of Betancí (Santos 1989). Such associations confirm archaeological data as to the relations that united Urabá, the Sinú River, the Darién of Panama, and the Colombian Pacific region for centuries without ever causing these different cultural areas to lose their local identities (see Bray 1984).

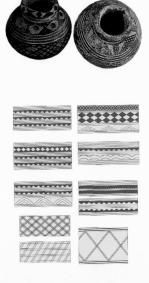

fig. **12**

THE DECORATIONS IN RED PAINT

on these Betancí vessels reproduce textile designs. Museo Sergio Restrepo S.J., Tierralta, Cordoba, Colombia. Photo Ana María Falchetti.

fig. **13**

THESE DESIGNS IN RED PAINT

decorate Zenú ceramic vessels in the modeled-and-painted tradition. Drawing by Melba Rodríguez de León.

The details of the symbolism of the ceramic female figures have been lost together with the Zenú mythology that explained them. Nevertheless, these clay women (abundant only in burials, which represent a return to Mother Earth) with their exaggerated sexual areas and occasionally carrying children, suggest fertility and the continuity of life. These concepts were recently alive and well in the funerary rites of the inhabitants of the San Andrés de Sotavento community, where the earth is conceived as the source of life to which all things return at the hour of death. Before covering the sepulcher with a mound of earth, mourners filled the grave with three layers of earth to be compacted by three two-and-three-quarter-yard long cylindrical wooden instruments known as *tampers*. "One male and two female *tampers* stepped on the dead," as they phrase it, in a rhythmic dance that symbolically relived the moment of fecunda-tion (see Turbay and Jaramillo 1986, 299).

It is possible that the ancient Zenúes wrapped their dead in their own hammocks, to judge from the survival of this tradition into recent times on the San Andrés de Sotavento reservation (Turbay and Jaramillo 1986, 301). This ritual could be related to the protective role assigned to textiles in situations that imply a change of state, death being seen as a transfor-mation toward rebirth (see Osborn 1995, 78; Falchetti 1997b). Funerary urns could similarly symbolize a return to the uterus. This was a fre-quent association for ceramic vessels, which are, after all, where the transformation of foodstuffs takes place, a process intrinsic to embryonic development (see Osborn 1995, 60). The urns were not commonly found among the Zenúes,

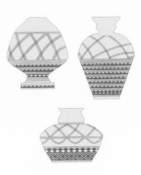

fig. **14**

THE DECORATION IN RED PAINT
*on these vessels
in the modeled-and-painted tradition
reproduces textile designs.
Drawing by Melba Rodríguez de León.*

although they were used in the lower Sinú and in the intermediate zone between this river and the San Jorge. The recent find of a ceramic female figure buried in a funerary urn[5] is especially suggestive in this symbolic context.

We know from the Spanish chronicles that the Zenúes of the sixteenth century main-tained an intense ceremonial activity that included pilgrimages to special sanctuaries like the one at Finzenú. A temple there was guarded by *mohanes* while wooden statues of men and women supported the hammock on which the Zenúes deposited gold offerings. This hammock appears to have symbolized the place of rest of a specific deity:

. . . the devil's hut, where a very elaborate hammock was placed . . . and atop the hammock, where they said the devil came to rest, were the two habas [baskets with gold offerings] (Friede 1956, vol. 6, 216).

Also located at Finzenú was a necropolis where *caciques* and *mohanes* were buried during the course of communal events that brought together the populations of vast terri-tories. The same divinities were worshipped at temples in Finzenú and Faraquiel, possibly on the upper Sinú (Simón 1625/1981, vol. 5, 128). Large mound cemeteries found in other areas also show the regional importance of a single system of beliefs. Fragments of Zenú tradition recovered by Spanish chroniclers describe the cultural and ideological identity of the peoples who participated in those pilgrimages and rituals:

[The *cacique* Zenufana] . . . *ordered the greatest of the lords of the other two Zenúes to be buried in this, his sister's Zenú [Finzenú], together with all the gold which they possessed at the hour of death, according to their custom, or at least that they maintain marked graves in the cemetery of the great sanctuary and the devil's hut in this Finzenú . . . and that if they did not want to be buried in them, that they should at least send half of the gold they would have at the hour of their death to bury in their stead in their marked grave* (Simón 1625/1981, vol. 5, 98).

Archaeological research in the San Jorge River basin demonstrates that mound graves were built for many centuries after these regions were first occupied by the ancestors of the Zenúes. There was a social differentiation among funerary practices. Tombs raised on the border of the thousands of artificial house platforms probably indicate family burials. Cemeteries containing only small tombs—with few offerings in ceramic, gold, or stone—contrast greatly with those dedicated to large mounds of up to six feet in height that hold many gold and ceramic pieces (Plazas et al. 1993). A single mound might include multiple burials, presumably of important individuals. At the great tumulus of Finzenú, called the "Sepulcher of the Devil" by the Spanish, many of the priests of the Zenúes were buried (Simón 1625/1981, vol. 5, 109). The movement of objects from different regions for burial in special sites is confirmed by findings at the Planeta Rica tombs, located in the intermediate zone between the Sinú and San Jorge rivers. Ceramic pieces originating at the basins of both rivers have been found there (ICAN 1994, 87-98; Falchetti 1995, 216, 268).

In modeled-and-painted ceramics a certain distinction between funerary and domestic vessels is observed. In some dwellings an abundance of fragments of simple culinary vessels have been found: large wide-mouthed vessels for storage, cups for serving food, and receptacles with necks for liquids (Plazas and Falchetti, 1981; Plazas et al. 1993, 203). Some domestic vessels decorated with modeled ornamentation or geometric designs in red paint were used as funerary offerings on some occasions, but certain forms were used exclusively for ceremonial functions. During communal funerary ceremonies gold objects, ceramics, and other items might be produced for interment in the tombs later in the rites. In Finzenú during the sixteenth century, for example, a community of goldsmiths made pieces "on order" (Aguado 1581/1957, vol. 4, 21). The female figures and other ceramics of the San Jorge River bring to mind this sort of immediate production of objects

161.

162.

OCARINA: FANGED FELINE

Small figural whistles and *ocarinas* were cherished by the Tairona, as is evident from the detail lavished on them. By late Tairona times a profuse use of incising as decoration was characteristic of these masterful works of art. This form of *ocarina* is characterized by dual sonic chambers. The central motif, which may be anthropomorphic or zoomorphic, is usually situated between the two chambers. Undoubtedly, *ocarinas* such as this were ritual objects, rather than toys. Tairona region. Late Tairona style. Ca. A.D. 1000-1600. Black pottery. 3" h. x 2⅞" w. Private collection

ZOOMORPHIC FIGURE WITH OPEN MOUTH

The large bold zones of black and red-brown and the sharp contours of the mouth suggest that this figure is rendered in the Piartal rather than the Capulí style although the primary colors are typical of the Capulí style. The figure combines the stylized head of a frog, the arms and legs of a man, and the tail of a monkey, implying the figure's shamanic affiliations. The open mouth, upward angled head, and stout stomach suggest a petition to the sky for rain, a common motif in southern Nariño. Highland Nariño region, Department of Nariño. Piartal style. Ca. A.D. 750-1200. Pottery with black on red-brown slip. 6" h. x 4½" w. Private collection. Publications: Labbé 1986, no. 122; Labbé 1988, no. 122.

of transitory function: made of fragile paste that is scarcely fired, these objects give the impression of having been made exclusively to be deposited in these sepulchers. The basket-shaped receptacles (cat. no. 147), with their complex form, excessive weight, and unstable base, must have had that function, as did the large-stemmed cups from Betancí, which were decorated with a great number of cut designs (cat. no. 149). On the other hand, it is also possible that these pieces were used for temple rituals like the figurines and the cups with covers (fig. 9) found in the San Jorge River area. The latter contain a calcareous substance in their interior—possibly used in chewing coca—and their decoration, confined to only one side of the vessel, suggests that they were placed on a fixed spot, to be seen exclusively from one direction.

Naturalism predominates in Zenú ceramics. While the human figure is most common, there are some animal representations like that of the jaguar in catalogue number 147 or the armadillo on the cover of a Betancí cup (cat. no. 149). There are also figures that show the union of man and animal—a representation of shamanic transformation—such as jaguars that frequently wear diadems, nose rings, and other ornaments that reveal them as men who have undergone transformation.

Ceremonial scenes are also represented. Music, which as ritual language must have been an essential part of ceremonies, and ritual beverages are alluded to in some Betancí vessels and in gold objects. Musicians may hold wind instruments and *maracas* in their hands while women carry a vessel (fig. 10), possibly the gourd bowl known as *totuma*, filled with *chicha*, a fermented beverage made of corn. In the funerary rites of the ancient Zenúes, the size of the tomb built depended not only on the importance of the deceased but also on the length of time the *chicha* lasted during the ceremony (Simón 1625/1981, vol. 5, 105-106, 128). The corn was stored in "granaries" in the *cacique's* home, since it was his responsibility to accumulate products to be redistributed later during communal rites.

fig. 16
SINU HATS,
produced by the inhabitants
of the San Andrés de Sotavento Indian
reservation, are part of a textile
tradition that goes back to the
ancient Zenú people. Their designs
reproduce animals, plants, and objects
commonly used by the community.
Photo Ana María Falchetti.

In many indigenous societies, corn is the sacred seed. *Chicha* is the offering par excellence, since the seed is considered to be transformed into a germ of life when the women chew it in order to liquify it (Osborn 1995). Among the Emberas of west Colombia, the women still make *chicha*, considered the essence of manhood, the beverage that makes man godlike (Vasco 1987, 90). Because the female is related to the notion of origins, female figures represent ancestors on some Embera ceramics (Vasco 1987, 91). The Zenúes may have held similar ideas for many of their ceramics showing female figures and wide-mouthed globular vessels—probably made to ferment and contain *chicha*—have survived. These vessels are decorated with female figures in Betancí examples (cat. no. 54). In Betancí burial plots, large pots have been found (Reichel-Dolmatoff 1957) with forms that have traditionally been used for *chicha* on the present-day San Andrés de Sotavento reservation. According to the chronicles of the Spanish conquest, Zenúes of the Sinú River basin and the surrounding areas placed vessels with *chicha* and foodstuff for the afterlife inside their tombs.

ZOOMORPHIC VESSEL

163.
The black slip, fine detail, and sharpness of line are all characteristic of later Tairona blackware. The feline is closely associated with shamanism among the Kogi who are descended from the ancient Tairona. On one level of meaning the jaguar symbolizes raw sexual energy that must be mediated and placed under cultural control by means of ritual. Tairona region. Late Tairona style. Ca. A.D. 1000-1600. Mottled black pottery. 7¾" h. x 9¼" l. Private collection

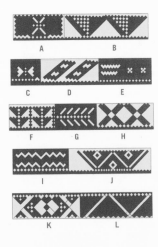

fig. **17**

DESIGNS THAT DECORATE SINÚ HATS,
*produced today at the San Andrés
de Sotavento Indian reservation
in the north of Colombia.
(A) praying mantis, (B) beehive, (C) wasp,
(D) snake, (E) rabbit footprint,
(F) butterflies, (G) fishbone, (H) tortoise,
(I) turtle, (J) snake, (K) toad, (L) snake.
Drawing by Melba Rodríguez de León.*

The Embera believe that clay, a mixture of earth and water, is the primordial union through which humans were created. Pottery, clay that has been fired for utilitarian purposes, is also identified with burnt "feline meat," for vessels with feline figures are nothing less than the animal hardened by fire (Vasco 1987). This concept also reminds us of the Zenúes, people of earth and water whose ceramics celebrate the feline as the predominant animal. One of these figures is of great size (fig. 11). The animal might appear in a dominant position either on the edge or on the cover of receptacles to be buried in tombs (cat. no. 147).

The influence of textiles is clearly evident in Zenú pottery. This should not be surprising, since pottery and textiles are tightly linked not only in the daily life of indigenous people but also in their myths. The Emberas, for example, mythically establish the common origin of baskets and pitchers and their relation to the production and transformation of foodstuff (Vasco 1987, 145).

In Zenú modeled-and-painted ceramics this association is observed in the elaborate "baskets" (cat. no. 147), the "fringes" that adorn some vessels, and geometric decoration in reddish paint, whether monochrome or bichrome, that also appears on the globular Betancí receptacles (fig. 12). Typically, the lower part has a loose weave that represents a net with oblique parallel lines, and the upper part has intercalated horizontal lines with rows of triangles or rhomboids to reproduce the closely woven designs of textiles (figs. 13, 14; Plazas et al. 1993,

BIRD-SHAPED NOSE ORNAMENT

This elaborate ornament is fashioned from embossed sheet gold decorated with repoussé designs. Cylindrical and round danglers are attached with wire strips. The ornament appears to represent a bird with wings outstretched. In actual use, light would have glimmered off of each dangler. Department of Valle del Cauca. Yotoco style. A.D. 1-800. Gold. 5⅞" h. x 6½" w. Museo del Oro (5403)

164.

BOWL: BIRDS

The design consists of a central tondo encircled by a primary decorative band consisting of a series of paired black and white birds. The white birds result from negative space created by the configuration of the black birds. The long beaks of the white birds extend into the bodies of the black birds. Both black and white birds share an eye and head. The beaks of the black birds are short while those of the white birds are long. White is a color associated with males in pre-Columbian iconography, particularly when contrasted with black. The long beak is also associated with the male gender, again particularly since it is contrasted with the short beaks of the black birds. The gender symbolism, with strong fertility connotations, is reinforced by the fact that the long beak of the white birds penetrates and extends into the bodies of the black birds. Highland Nariño region, Department of Nariño. Tuza style. A.D. 1250-1500. Pottery with black and red on white slip. 3⅜" h. x 6⅜" d. Private collection

165.

109-11). The influence of textiles is also evident in Zenú metalwork in which the distinctive use of cast filigree constitutes a veritable metal weave. It was used to make the ear ornaments (fig. 15) characteristic of Zenú goldwork and to decorate other ornaments.

The ancient importance of textiles is evident in the diadems, visors, and hats used by the personages represented in metal staff heads. This tradition has been passed down through the centuries and is manifest today in the Sinú hat (fig. 16), which is made from the cane fiber *fleche* (*Gynerium saccharoides*) in the San Andrés de Sotavento communities. The hat is fashioned of thin strips of fiber—some white and others dyed black with *bija* (*Arrhabidea chica*)—intercalated to make long "braids" with geometric designs that are then sewn together (Leroy Gordon 1986, 304-41; Turbay and Jaramillo 1983, 128-29). Traditionally, different towns specialized in different stages of the manufacture of the hat and in its distinctive decorative designs, such as the abstractions of plants, animals or parts of them, and objects (figs. 17, 18), and inherited the right to make particular designs through a matrilineal line (Turbay and Jaramillo 1986, 344-49, 432). This tradition helps us understand the past organization of both textile manufacturing and ceramics production, both of which display standardized patterns, as well as regional differences.

Today's hat designs recall those of modeled-and-painted ceramics of prehispanic times with their characteristic combinations of triangles, rhomboids, and parallel lines. Certain decorative motifs used in hats today might have had symbolic strength in the past, but while the names of the designs have endured, their symbolism has progressively disappeared (Turbay and Jaramillo 1986, 344-49; Turbay 1993).

Villages on the San Andrés reservation have traditionally specialized in different sorts of production. While some concentrate on hatmaking, others are known for producing pottery or for making cotton hammocks (Leroy Gordon 1957; Turbay and Jaramillo 1986). The origins of this sectored specialization go back to the ancient Zenúes.

BOWL: FIGURE WITH BIRDS

166. Piartal-style designs usually cover the entire decorative field and are not characterized by a central tondo or encircling decorative bands as in the Tuza style. This design appears to consist of a human figure carrying a pole, on which two birds are perched. Closer observation, however, reveals a skillfully contrasted positive and negative design and a number of forms arranged yin-yang fashion to imbue the composition with powerful fertility imagery. The serpentine-shaped pathway is decorated with a series of red ovals, possibly representing seeds or eggs. The geometric design below the pathway consists of four geometric birds arranged as complementary pairs. These white geometric birds result as negative space against the positive black background. The black paint overlays the white paint. Highland Nariño region, Department of Nariño. Piartal style. Ca. A.D. 750-1250. Pottery with black and red on white slip. 3¼" h. x 8⅜" d. Private collection

FOOTED BOWL: DEER AND FELINES ENCIRCLING THE SUN

167. Tuza bowls are often characterized by a central tondo encircled by a main decorative band. The tondo is decorated with a design element that represents the sun. The main decorative band comprises a series of alternating deer and felines, all but one of which have birds on their backs. The cross elements in the background most likely represent stars. The pattern of felines and deer represents alternation of predator and prey, a scenario that has astronomical or astrological significance. Highland Nariño region, Department of Nariño. Tuza style. Ca. A.D. 1250-1500. Pottery with black paint on white slip. 3¼" h. x 7⅜" d. Private collection

201.

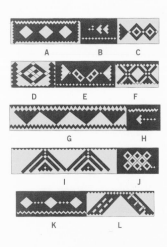

fig. **18**

SINÚ HAT DESIGNS.

(A) drums, (B) fly, (C) chicken's eye,
(D) turkey, (E) mortar,
(F) spider, (G) comb, (H) footpath,
(I) comb, (J) sieve,
(K) necklace, (L) orange blossom.
Drawing by Melba Rodríguez de León.

Like goldsmiths, potters may have occupied an important social position. Through the use of fire, they had the power to transform special materials into objects of social significance. For this reason, their craft has been surrounded by myths, taboos, and rituals in numerous societies (see Lévi-Strauss 1986). We may glean certain beliefs of this sort from potters in the San Andrés community, who still conserve their traditions: fresh bowls cannot be looked at or touched by menstruating women, and the sand that is mixed with the clay must be extracted from a local creek, free of animal excrement, and specially cleaned (Turbay and Jaramillo 1986, 258). Such restrictions recall the beliefs common to many peoples regarding the "contamination" of raw materials that can damage the final product and bring danger to the community. Today, as in the past, it is the women who make pottery on the reservation. Perhaps, as happens in many other societies, the ceramic vessel is associated with women because of their link to procreation and to the transformations that can take place within the clay receptacles (Osborn 1979, 60).

CERAMICS AND IDENTITY

Ceramics, like other items of manufacture, have expressed through time the particularism of Zenú society, differentiating it from other communities of strong character that occupied the Caribbean plains. The Malibúes of the Lower Magdalena River established important population centers on the river banks and neighboring marshes without making any artificial modifications for housing, burial, or drainage as did the Zenúes. Archaeologists have established that Malibú influence dates from the fourteenth century in regions previously occupied by the Zenúes in the Lower San Jorge River (Plazas and Falchetti 1981; Plazas et al. 1993). The settlements of two different ethnic groups have been identified through contrasts in environmental adaptation, housing sites, funerary customs, and material culture, especially in ceramics.

Malibú pottery differs from that of the Zenúes in several ways: it is resistant, well fired, has utilitarian orientation, and exhibits a series of distinctive shapes decorated with incised geometric patterns. With the possible exception of flutes (cat. no. 65) and certain small vessels (cat. no. 29), ritual or exclusively funerary forms are not common. Rather, utilitarian vessels were reconditioned for these uses: large globular bowls were used as funerary urns, especially in the burial of children, and small bowls and cups with long stems made up the funerary offerings (Plazas and Falchetti 1981, 115).

No real contact has yet been detected between the Zenúes and the Malibúes, but it is supposed that some Zenú communities remained in the flood areas when the Malibúes appeared. That possible contact is indicated in hybrid aspects of goldwork (Falchetti 1995, 292) and in those ceramic pieces that combine the solidity, elegance, and incised decoration of the Malibú tradition with the sculptural tendencies that distinguish the pottery of the Zenúes (cat. no. 17).

These stylistic clues reinforce the archaeological and ethnohistorical data that establishes both the presence of different ethnic groups on the plains of the Colombian Caribbean and the production by these groups of ceramics that reflect their respective customs and beliefs. In the case of the Zenúes, we believe that the locations and products of the various manufacturing centers underwent continual change. This continuity and adaptability would explain in part the abundance of pieces and the makeup of different ceramic groups in different regions and epochs that never lost the distinctive Zenú mark, a characteristic that tends to affirm the existence of a long tradition linked to communities able to maintain a traditional ethnic identity.

NOTES

1 They belong to the granular-and-incised tradition. The oldest recorded date for this pottery, corresponding to the second century before Christ, was obtained in the Lower San Jorge River area (Plazas et al. 1993, 61, 80).

2 They belong to the local group referred to as the Carate-Parajal Complex and, according to dates available today, were produced between the third and ninth centuries (Plazas et al. 1993, 61, 81).

3 The gold pieces belong to the San Jorge-Cauca Group, one of the Zenú goldwork groups that developed in large areas of the Lower San Jorge and Lower Cauca rivers (Falchetti 1993; Falchetti 1995, 223-36).

4 A group of metal pieces found in the coastal zone between Urabá and the mouth of the Sinú River included a multiple zoomorphic pendant together with pieces related to Zenú goldwork that were dated to the thirteenth century. The date was obtained from the clay and carbon core preserved in one of these pieces (Museo del Oro, 33459; Beta 82926. 670 ± 70 B.P.; Plazas and Archila 1997).

5 Recently acquired by Santafé de Bogotá's Museo del Oro (Juanita Sáenz Samper, personal communication).

glossary

ADORNO   A small figure or ornament cast or modeled individually and attached as decoration to a vessel or other form.

ALCARRAZA   A basic jar form characterized by two vertical attenuated spouts joined by a strap or bridge handle.

AMPHORA   A basic vessel form characterized by an ovoid body and a distinct neck. The bases of such vessels are often conical and the necks long and cylindrical.

APPLIQUÉD   Decorated through the application of fillets or other adornments modeled or formed separately.

ATLANTEAN   A term describing figures that support other forms.

CACICA   A female leader or ruler.

CACIQUE   A male leader or ruler; a chieftain.

CANASTERO   A genre found in the Calima region. Characterized by an anthropomorphic or zoomorphic figure in crouched position, with a hollow receptacle at the back.

CARINATED   Having a characteristic ridge formed by the point of contact of two sloping or inclined surfaces.

CAYMAN   A South American crocodilian.

CERAMIC   Clay that is fired at relatively high temperatures.

CERAMIC TRADITION   A classificatory category embracing a number of related ceramic wares.

CERAMIC TYPE   Usually a regional or local variant and subdivision of ceramic ware.

CERAMIC WARE   A classificatory category that is a subdivision of a tradition embracing a number of related ceramic forms. Characterized by similarities in surface treatment, core type, and technique of manufacture.

CHICHA   An alcoholic beverage made from fermented corn.

CROSSHATCHED   Decorated with parallel lines crossed by other parallel lines and resulting in series of squares or diamond-shaped patterns.

DIMORPHIC   Having two distinct forms for one class of objects or species of life.

EMBOSSED   Characterized by raised designs produced by pressing or hammering the design on the reverse side of the work. In this publication *embossed* is used as a synonym for *repoussé*.

FOOTED   Characterized by a short supporting disc or other structural element.

HATCHED   Decorated with parallel lines used as shading.

INCENSARIO   A vessel used to contain burning incense.

INCISED   Characterized by designs produced by cutting into the work with a sharp instrument.

LABRET   An ornament placed in a specially prepared hole in the lower lip.

MESOAMERICA The region extending from northern Mexico to the Gulf of Nicoya in Costa Rica.

METATE A stone slab used for grinding corn.

MÚCURA A basic Muisca vessel form characterized by a globular body, a relatively tall, narrow, cylindrical spout, and a handle connecting the spout to the body of the vessel.

OCARINA As found in Colombia, a wind instrument with multiple holes used to vary pitch and tone, differing from a flute in shape and by the fact that the player usually blows across the blowhole rather than into it.

OLLA A basic vessel form characterized by a globular body and a wide mouth.

PEDESTALED Having a supporting element characterized by a base and stem.

POPORO A vessel used to contain lime, used in chewing coca leaf.

POTTERY Clay that is fired at relatively low temperatures.

PUNCTATE Decorated with impressed points.

QUECHUA A major South American language spoken by the Inca and other indigenous peoples.

REPOUSSÉ See *embossed*.

RETABLO A popular term used in Colombia to refer to a genre of figures made in antiquity in the Middle Cauca region in which the body of the figure is made from a solid slab of clay and the limbs of solid tubes of clay.

SHAMAN A term applied to a religious functionary within certain indigenous societies worldwide. Shamans adhere to an ancient tradition possibly many thousands of years old. In the New World shamans are often believed capable of transforming their souls into various animal forms including the jaguar. They are also said to be able to travel out of their bodies ("soul flight"). The shaman mediates the forces of good and evil and is responsible for safeguarding the environment and ecosystem and assuring the fertility of man, plant, and animal.

SHOULDERED Having a distinct structural form curving outward from the base of the neck toward the middle of the body of a vessel.

SLIP A fine solution of clay applied to the surface of a pre-fired clay vessel or sculpture in order to create a smooth surface. The color of a fired slip is in large measure determined by firing.

SOLAR DEITY Among most indigenous cultures in Colombia the sun was believed to be a living being responsible for assuring life on earth. Some groups, however, distinguished between the ordinary physical sun and the sun as solar deity whose true self existed in an invisible dimension.

STEMMED Having a supporting column that attenuates away from a wide base.

TONDO A distinctly demarcated circular area found at the center of the inner surface of decorated bowls or cups.

TUMBAGA An alloy of copper and gold.

ZOOMORPHIC Having an animal-like form.

references

ARMAND J. LABBÉ

Archila, Sonia. 1996. *Los Tesoros de los Señores de Malagana*. Santafé de Bogotá, Colombia: Museo del Oro, Banco de la República.

Arte de la Tierra, Colombia: Muiscas y Guanes. 1989. Colección Tesoros Precolombinos. Santafé de Bogotá, Colombia: Fondo de Promoción de la Cultura, Banco Popular.

Arte de la Tierra, Colombia: Quimbayas. 1990. Colección Tesoros Precolombinos. Santafé de Bogotá, Colombia: Fondo de Promoción de la Cultura, Banco Popular.

Arte de la Tierra, Colombia: Forma y Figura. 1992. Colección Tesoros Precolombinos. Santafé de Bogotá, Colombia: Fondo de Promoción de la Cultura, Banco Popular.

Arte de la Tierra, Colombia: Sinú y Río Magdalena. 1992. Colección Tesoros Precolombinos. Santafé de Bogotá, Colombia: Fondo de Promoción de la Cultura, Banco Popular.

Arte de la Tierra: Cultura Tumaco. 1994. Colección Tesoros Precolombinos. Santafé de Bogotá, Colombia: Fondo de Promoción de la Cultura, Banco Popular.

Arte de la Tierra, Colombia: Podor. 1994. Colección Tesoros Precolombinos. Santafé de Bogotá, Colombia: Fondo de Promoción de la Cultura, Banco Popular.

Bernal Villegas, J.B.B., Ignacio, Brinceño Balcázar, and Ronald Duncan. 1993. *El Arte del Chamanismo, La Salud y La Vida Tumaco-La Tolita*. Santafé de Bogotá, Colombia: Instituto Colombiano de Cultura Hispánica, Publicaciones Universidad Javeriana.

Bray, Warwick M. 1978. *The Gold of El Dorado*. London: Times Books.

Donnan, Christopher B. 1992. *Ceramics of Ancient Peru*. Los Angeles: Fowler Museum of Cultural History, University of California.

Emboden, William. 1979. *Narcotic Plants: Hallucinogens, Stimulants, Inebriants, and Hypnotics, Their Origins and Uses*. New York: Collier Books.

Ereira, Alan. 1990. *The Elder Brothers*. New York: Vintage Books.

Falchetti, Ana María. 1995. *El Oro del Gran Zenú: Metalurgia Prehispánica en las Llanuras del Caribe Colombiano*. Santafé de Bogotá, Colombia: Colección Bibliográfica, Banco de la República.

Historia del Arte Colombiano. 1977. Vol. 2. Santafé de Bogotá, Colombia: Salvat Editores Colombiana, S.A.

Jones, Julie, and Warwick Bray. 1974. *El Dorado: The Gold of Ancient Colombia*. New York: The Center for Inter-American Relations and The American Federation of Arts.

Labbé, Armand J. 1982. *Man and Cosmos in Prehispanic Mesoamerica*. Santa Ana, California: Bowers Museum Foundation.

———. 1986. *Colombia Before Columbus: The People, Culture, and Ceramic Art of Prehispanic Colombia*. New York: Rizzoli International Publishers, Inc.

———. 1988. *Colombia Antes de Colón*. Santafé de Bogotá, Colombia: Carlos Valencia Editores.

———. 1992. *Images of Power*. Santa Ana, California: Cultural Arts Press.

———. 1995. *Guardians of the Life Stream: Shamans, Art and Power in Prehispanic Central Panamá*. Santa Ana, California: Cultural Arts Press.

Labbé, Armand J., ed. 1992. *Tribute to the Gods: Treasures of the Museo del Oro*. Santa Ana, California: Cultural Arts Press.

Langeback Rueda, Carl H. 1987. "La Cronología de la Región Arqueológica Tairona Vista Desde Paparé, Municipio de Cienaga." *Boletín de Arqueología* (Santafé de Bogotá, Colombia) (January), no. 1: 83-101.

Lathrap, Donald W. 1975. *Ancient Ecuador: Culture, Clay and Creativity, 3000- 300 B.C.* Chicago: Field Museum of Natural History.

Levi-Strauss, Claude. 1955. *Saudades Do Brasil: A Photographic Memoir.* Seattle and London: University of Washington Press.

McDowell, John Holmes 1989. *Sayings of the Ancestors: The Spiritual Life of the Sibundoy Indians.* Lexington, Kentucky: The University Press of Kentucky.

Osborn, Ann. 1995. *Las Cuatro Estaciones: Mitología y estructura social entre los U'wa.* Santafé de Bogotá, Colombia: Museo del Oro, Banco de la República.

Oyuela-Caycedo, Augusto. 1986. "De Los Taironas A Los Kogi: Una interpretación del cambio cultural by Augusto Oyuela-Caycedo." *Museo del Oro, Boletín* (Santafé de Bogotá, Colombia), no. 17: 35.

———. 1995. *The Emergence of Pottery.* Washington, D.C.: Smithsonian Institution Press.

Perrin, Michel. 1992. *Les Praticiens Du Rêve: Un Exemple De Chamanisme.* Paris: Presses Universitaires de France.

Pineda Camacho, R. 1994. "Los Bancos Taumaturgos." *Museo del Oro, Boletín* (Santafé de Bogotá, Colombia), no. 36: 3-41.

Plazas, Clemencia, Ana María Falchetti, Juanita Sáenz Samper, and Sonia Archila. 1993. *La sociedad hidráulica Zenú. Estudio arqueológico de 2,000 años de historia en las llanuras del Caribe colombiano.* Santafé de Bogotá, Colombia: Museo del Oro, Banco de la República.

Reichel-Dolmatoff, Gerardo. 1950-51. *Los Kogi: Una Tribu Indígena de la Sierra Nevada de Santa Marta.* Santafé de Bogotá, Colombia: Instituto Etnológico Nacional, Editorial Iqueima.

———. 1971. *Amazonian Cosmos: The Sexual and Religious Symbolism of the Tukano Indians.* Chicago: University of Chicago Press.

———. 1975. *The Shaman and the Jaguar: A Study of Narcotic Drugs Among the Indians of Colombia.* Philadelphia: Temple University Press.

———. 1982. "Astronomical Models of Social Behavior Among Some Indians of Colombia." In *Ethnoastronomy and Archaeoastronomy in the American Tropics,* vol. 385, pp. 165-82. Eds. Anthony F. Aveni and Gary Urton. New York: Annals of The New York Academy of Sciences.

———. 1986. *Arqueología De Colombia: Un Texto Introductorio.* Santafé de Bogotá, Colombia: Colombia Funbotánica.

———. 1988. *Goldwork and Shamanism.* Medellín, Colombia: Compañía Litográfica Nacional, S.A.

Rojas de Perdomo, Lucia. 1995. *Arqueología Colombiana: Visión Panorámica.* Santafé de Bogotá, Colombia: Intermedio Editores, Circulo de Lectores S.A.

Rouse. Irving. 1972. *The Tainos: Rise and Decline of the People Who Greeted Columbus.* New Haven and London: Yale University Press.

Cardale de Schrimpff, Marianne, Warwick Bray, Theres Gähwiler-Walder, and Leonor Herrera. 1991. Calima: *Trois Cultures Précolombiennes dans le Sud-Ouest de la Colombie.* Lausanne: Editions Payot Lausanne.

Shimada, Izumi. 1994. *Tecnología y Organización de la Producción Cerámica Prehispánica en Los Andes.* Lima, Peru: Pontificia Universidad Católica del Perú, Fondo Editorial.

Wilbert, Johannes. 1993. *Mystic Endowment: Religious Ethnography of the Warao Indians.* Cambridge, Massachusetts: Harvard University Center for the Study of World Religions.

———. 1996. *Mindful of Famine: Religious Climatology of the Warao Indians.* Cambridge, Massachusetts: Harvard University Press for the Harvard University Center for the Study of World Religions.

Zerries, Otto. 1981. "Atributos e Instrumentos do Sul náo-andina e seu significado." In *Contirubuicóes a Antropología em homenagem ao prof. Egon Schaden,* pp. 319-60. Sáo Paulo, Brazil: Colecáo Museu Paulista.

WARWICK BRAY ET AL.

Archila, Sonia. 1996. *Los Tesoros de los Señores de Malagana*. Santafé de Bogotá, Colombia: Museo del Oro, Banco de la República.

Botiva Contreras, Alvaro, and Eduardo Forero Lloreda. 1994. "Malagana: Guaquería Vs. Arqueología." *Museo del Oro, Boletín* (Santafé de Bogotá, Colombia) 31 : 124-29.

Bray, Warwick. 1978 *The Gold of El Dorado*. London: Times Books.

————. 1992. "El Periodo Yotoco." In Marianne Cardale de Schrimpff, Warwick Bray, Theres Gähwiler-Walder, and Leonor Herrera, *Calima: Diez mil años de historia en el suroc cidente de Colombia*, pp. 75-124. Santafé de Bogotá, Colombia: Fundación Pro Calima.

Bray, Warwick, and Michael Edward Moseley. 1971. "An Archaeological Sequence from the Region of Buga, Colombia." *Ñawpa Pacha* 7-8: 85-103.

Cubillos Ch., Julio César. 1984. Arqueología del Valle del Rio Cauca. *Asentamientos Prehispánicos en la Suela Plana del Río Cauca*. Santafé de Bogotá, Colombia: Fundación de Investigaciones Arqueológicas Nacionales, Banco de la República.

Duque Gomez, Luis. 1979. "La Pieza del Museo." *Museo del Oro, Boletín,* (Santafé de Bogotá, Colombia) (May-August)

Ford, James A. 1944. "Excavations in the Vicinity of Cali, Colombia." *Yale University Publications in Anthropology* 30.

Gnecco, Cristóbal, and José Ricardo Martínez. 1995. "Dos alcarrazas Ilama en Tierradentro." *Museo del Oro, Boletín* (Santafé de Bogota, Colombia), nos. 32-33: 178-81.

Herrera, Leonor, Marianne Cardale de Schrimpff, and Warwick Bray. 1994. "Los sucesos de Malagana vistos desde Calima. Atando cabos en la arqueología del surocci dente colom- biano." *Revista Colombiana de Antropología* (Santafé de Bogotá, Colombia) 31: 145-74.

Herrera, Leonor, Marianne Cardale de Schrimpff, and Carlos Armando Rodríguez. 1994. "El proyecto arqueológico Malagana."

Revista Colombiana de Antropología (Santafé de Bogotá, Colombia) 31: 265-70

Lehmann, Henri. 1959. *Les Céramiques Précolombiennes*. Paris: Presses Universitaires de France.

Ortiz, George. 1996. *In Pursuit of the Absolute: Art of the Ancient World in the George Ortiz Collection* (revised edition). Berlin: Alter Museum.

Pérez de Barradas, José. 1954. *Orfebrería Prehispánica de Colombia: Estilo Calima*. Madrid: Jura.

Plazas, Clemencia, and Ana María Falchetti. 1983. "Tradición Metalúrgica del Suroccidente Colombiano." *Museo del Oro, Boletín* (Santafé de Bogotá, Colombia) 14: 1-32.

————. 1985. "Cultural Patterns in Prehispanic Goldwork from Colombia." In *The Art of Precolumbian Gold: The Jan Mitchell Collection*, pp. 47-59. Ed. Julie Jones. London: Weidenfeld and Nicolson.

————. 1986. "Patrones culturales en la orfebrería prehispánica de Colombia." In *Metalurgia en América Precolombina*, pp. 210-46. Ed. Clemencia Plazas. Santafé de Bogotá, Colombia: Banco de la República.

Reichel-Dolmatoff, Gerardo. 1965. *Colombia*. London: Thames and Hudson.

Rodríguez, Carlos Armando. 1992. *Tras las Huellas del Hombre Prehispánico y su Cultura en el Valle del Cauca*. Cali, Colombia: Instituto Vallecaucano de Investigaciones Científicas.

Rodríguez, Carlos Armando, Leonor Herrera Angel, and Marianne Cardale de Schrimpff. 1993. "El Proyecto Arqueológico Malagana (1994)." *Boletín de Arqueología* (Santafé de Bogotá, Colombia) 8, no. 3: 59-70.

Rodríguez, Carlos Armando, and David Michael Stemper. 1994. "Cambios Medioambientales y Culturales Prehispánicos en el Curso Bajo del río Bolo, municipio de Palmira, Valle del Cauca." *Cespedesia* (Cali, Colombia) 19, nos. 62-63: 139-98.

Cardale Schrimpff [in Spanish, Cardale de Schrimpff], Marianne. 1989. "The Snake and the Fabulous Beast: Themes from the Pottery

of the Ilama Culture." In *Animals into Art.*
Ed. Howard Morphy. *One World Archaeology*
(London), no. 7: 75-106.

———. 1992a. "La Gente del Periodo Ilama."
In Marianne Cardale de Schrimpff, Warwick
Bray, Theres Gähwiler-Walder, and Leonor
Herrera, *Calima: Diez mil años de historia en el
suroccidente de Colombia,* pp. 25-71. Santafé de
Bogotá, Colombia: Fundación Pro Calima.

———. 1992b. "Basketry in the Northern Andes
and Intermontane Valleys of Colombia." In
*Basketmakers, Meaning and Form in Native
American Baskets,* pp. 113-29. Eds. Linda
Mowat, Howard Morphy, and Penny Dransart.
Oxford: Pitt Rivers Museum Monograph No. 5.

———. 1996. *Caminos Prehispánicos de Colombia.
El estudio de caminos precolombinos en la
cuenca del alto río Calima, Cordillera Occidental,
Valle del Cauca.* Santafé de Bogotá, Colombia:
Fundación de Investigaciones Arqueólogicas
Nacionales, Banco de la República y
Fundación Pro Calima.

ANA MARÍA FALCHETTI

Aguado, Fray Pedro de [1581] 1957. *Recopilación
Historial.* Santafé de Bogotá, Colombia:
Biblioteca de la Presidencia de Colombia.

Bray, Warwick. 1984. "Across the Darien Gap:
A Colombian View of Isthmian Archeology."
The Archeology of Lower Central America.
Eds. F.W. Lange and D.Z. Stone. School of
American Research Advanced Seminar
Series. Albuquerque: University of New
Mexico Press.

Briones de Pedraza, Bartolomé. [1580] 1983.
"Relación de Tenerife II." *Cespedesia* (Cali,
Colombia), nos. 45-46, suppl. no. 4.

Castellanos, Juan de. [1601] 1955. *Elegias de
Varones Ilustres de Indias.* Vol. 3. Santafé de
Bogotá, Colombia: Biblioteca de la
Presidencia de Colombia. Editorial ABC.

Falchetti, Ana María. 1993. "La tierra del oro y
el cobre: parentesco e intercambio entre
comunidades orfebres del norte de Colombia
y áreas relacionadas." *Museo del Oro, Boletín*
(Santafé de Bogotá, Colombia), nos. 34-35.

———. 1995. *El Oro del Gran Zenú: Metalurgia
Prehispánica en las llanuras del Caribe
Colombiano.* Santafé de Bogotá, Colombia:
Colección Bibliográfica, Banco de la
República.

———. 1997a. "El territorio del Gran Zenú en
las llanuras del Caribe colombiano.
Arqueología y Etnohistoria." *Revista de
Arqueología Americana* (Mexico), no. 11: 7-41.

———. 1997b. *La Ofrenda y la Semilla. Notas
sobre el simbolismo del oro entre los Uwa.*
49° Congreso Internacional de Americanistas
(Metalurgia de América Prehispánica).
Quito, Ecuador.

Friede, Juan. 1956. *Documentos inéditos para la
Historia de Colombia.* Vols. 3, 4, 5. Madrid:
Academia Colombiana de Historia, Artes
Gráficas.

———. 1960. *Documentos inéditos para la
Historia de Colombia.* Vols. 7, 8. Madrid:
Academia Colombiana de Historia, Artes
Gráficas.

Herrera, Leonor, and Marianne Cardale de
Schrimpff. 1974. "Mitología Cuna: Los Kalu,
según Don Alfonso Díaz Granados." *Revista
Colombiana de Antropología* (Santafé de
Bogotá, Colombia) 17: 201-247.

ICAN, COLCULTURA, Oleoducto de Colombia.
1994. *Arquelogía de Rescate. Un viaje por el
tiempo a largo del oleoducto.* (Trabajos
arquelógicos dirigidos por Alvaro Botiva).
Santafé de Bogotá, Colombia.

Le Roy Gordon, Bruce. 1957. *Human Geography
and Ecology in the Sinú Country of Colombia.*
Berkeley and Los Angeles: University of
California Press.

Lévi-Strauss, Claude. 1986. *La Alfarera Celosa.*
Barcelona: Paidos Studio Básica.

Morales, Jorge. 1997. *Oro, control al incesto y
cultura entre los Cuna* (Metalurgia Prehispánica
de América). 49° Congreso Internacional de
Americanistas. Quito, Equador.

Osborn, Ann. 1979. *La Cerámica de los Tunebos.
Un estudio etnográfico. Fundación de Investi-
gaciones Arquelógicas Nacionales.* Santafé de
Bogota, Colombia: Banco de la República.

———. 1995. *Las Cuatro Estaciones. Mitología y estructura social entre los U'wa*. Colección Bibliográfica. Santafé de Bogotá, Colombia: Banco de la República.

Plazas, Clemencia, and Sonia Archila. 1997. *Cronologia de la Metalurgia prehispánica de Colombia* (Metalurgia de América Prehispánica). 49° Congresso Internacional de Americanistas. Quito, Ecuador.

Plazas, Clemencia, and Ana María Falchetti. 1981. *Asentamientos Prehispánicos en el bajo río San Jorge*. Santafé de Bogotá: Colombia: Fundación de Investigaciones Arqueológicas Nacionales, Banco de la República.

———. 1986. "La cultura del oro y del agua. Un proyecto de reconstrucción." *Boletín Cultural y Bibliográfico* (Santafé de Bogotá, Colombia) 23, no. 6: 57-72.

———. 1990. "Manejo hidráulico Zenú." *Ingenierías Prehispánicas*. Santafé de Bogotá, Colombia: Fondo FEN Colombia, Instituto Colombiano de Antropología.

Plazas, Clemencia, Ana María Falchetti, Thomas van der Hammen, and Pedro Botero. 1988. "Cambios ambientales y desarrollo cultural en el bajo río San Jorge." *Museo del Oro, Boletín* (Santafé de Bogotá, Colombia), no. 20: 55-58.

Plazas, Clemencia, Ana María Falchetti, Juanita Sáenz Samper, and Sonia Archila. 1993. *La sociedad hidráulica Zenú. Estudio arqueológico de 2,000 años de historia en las llanuras del Caribe colombiano*. Santafé de Bogotá, Colombia: Museo del Oro, Banco de la República.

Reichel-Dolmatoff, Gerardo. 1981. *Things of Beauty Replete with Meaning: Metals and Crystals in Colombian Indian Cosmology*. Los Angeles: Natural History Museum of Los Angeles County.

Reichel-Dolmatoff, Gerardo and Alicia. 1957. "Reconocimiento arqueológico de la hoya del río Sinú." *Revista Colombiana de Antropología* (Santafé de Bogotá, Colombia) 6: 31-149.

Santos, Gustavo. 1989. "Las etnías indígenas prehispánicas y de la conquista en la región del Golfo de Urabá." *Boletín de Antropología* (Medellín, Colombia) 6, no. 22.

Sáenz Samper, Juanita. 1993. "Mujeres de barro. Estudio de las figurinas cerámicas de la región de Montelíbano, Córdoba." *Museo del Oro, Boletín* (Santafé de Bogotá, Colombia), nos. 34-35: 77- 109.

Simón, Fray Pedro [1625] 1981. *Noticias Historiales*. Santafé de Bogotá, Colombia: Biblioteca BancoPopular.

Turbay, Sandra. 1993. Croyances et pratiques religieuses des Zenus de la Plaine Caraibe Colombienne. Ph.D. diss. Ecole des Hautes Etudes en Sciences Sociales, Paris.

Turbay, Sandra, and Susana Jaramillo. 1986. La identidad cultural entre los indigenas de San Andrés de Sotavento. Thesis. Córdoba, Colombia. Universidad de Antioquia, Medellín.

Vargas, Patricia. 1993. *Los Emberas y los Cuna: impacto y reacción ante la ocupación española. Siglos XVI y XVIIU*. Santafé de Bogotá, Colombia: CEREC, Instituto Colombiano de Antropología.

Vasco, Luis Guillermo. 1987. *Semejantes a los Dioses. Cerámica y cestería embera-chamí*. Santafé de Bogotá, Colombia: Centro Editorial, Universidad Nacional de Colombia.

PHOTOGRAPH CREDITS

index

Boldface page numbers refer to catalogue text; *italic* page numbers refer to figures and their captions. Catalogue items are referenced by catalogue number (no.), not page number. Entries on style (e.g., "llama style") include references to the period and people who produced the style.

alcarrazas, 32, 86, **95, 103, 110, 128,** 143, 144, 148, 149, 152, 153, **167;** nos. 37, 41-42, 76, 81, 89, 91, 93, 112, 115-16, 118-19, 135
Amazon peoples, **27,** 53, **58,** 78, 116, **119, 168**
American Southwest, 18, 19, **116, 119**
animals, 104-16; mythical or fantastic, 147, 153, **167, 174;** no. 140; *see also* shamans: animal associations; zoomorphic representations; *for specific motifs, see* armadillo; bat; bird; butterfly; crab; crocodilian; deer; dragon; eagle; feline; frog; jaguar; monkey; owl; serpent; toad; turtle
anthropomorphic figures, 26, **32, 44, 99, 100,** 104, **174, 178**
anthropomorphized forms: flute, no. 65; pectorals, nos. 68-69, 77; pendants, nos. 58, 70-71; pole, no. 113; vessels, 78-93; nos. 17, 97-107, 109, 114; see also *canasteros*
armadillo motif, 108, **182,** 197; no. 149
astronomical motifs, 110-15, 116, **167, 191, 201**
Atlantean figures, 49, **174;** no. 143
Ayapel, 173
Aztecs, 22, **35,** 43, 100

Bachue, 19, 26, 86, 87, **131**
Baja Guajira region, 15, 26; nos. 36, 140
basketry, 149, 198
bat motif, 108, **110,** 143, 147, 148, **159, 171, 182, 185;** nos. 150, 152
beads, 135, 140, *140,* 142-43, *147,* 153; necklaces of, *148;* nos. 4, 63, 160
benches: with animal forms, **35,** 43, 44, **49;** figures seated on, 8, 21-22, 26, **27,** 27-40, **39, 40,** 43, 48, 49-53, **58, 61, 62,** 78, **99,** *110,* 182; nos. 1-3, 6-8, 11-12, 14-15, 26, 92; figure squatting on, *26,* 31; with offering, no. 29; of shamans, 27, 32, 44-48, 53, 182
Betancí modeled-and-incised style, 15,

36-40, 50, 58, 61, **67, 73, 77,** *178,* 172, *186,* 192, *192,* 195, 197, 198; nos. 44, 49, 54-55, 149
bird (avian) motifs, **31,** 44, **50, 57,** 68, 73, **92, 96,** 104, 108, 109, 116, **119, 136,** 144, 148, **167, 191, 198, 201;** nos. 95, 160, 164-66; *see also* eagle; owl
black pottery (blackware), 48, 50; nos. 6, 9, 12, 24, 26, 29, 47-48, 134, 141, 157, 161; mottled, no. 163
Bochica, 19, 26, 86, 87, **131**
body ornaments, 21; *see also* ear ornaments; labrets; nose ornaments; pectorals
Botero, Fernando, 61
Botiva, Alvaro, 126
bottle, *153,* 154; see also *alcarrazas*
bowls, 9, 78, 86, 87, *178;* nos. 96, 109, 132-33, 137, 143, 156, 165-66, 202; *alcarraza* in shape of, no. 112; figures holding, 53, **57,** 81; no. 59; footed, 104; no. 167; pedestal, nos. 49, 149
braid pattern, **48, 50, 185**
Bray, Warwick, 19, 121-54
breastplates, 143, *144,* 152, *172, 173,* 182, 186
brown incised style, 15
brown pottery (brownware), **96, 125, 144, 167;** nos. 13, 74, 132, 149, 151; cream-brown, no. 82; dark brown, nos. 75, 84, 156; grey-brown, nos. 7, 78, 117, 146; light brown, nos. 44, 49, 55, 103, 106, 121, 159; mottled brown, nos. 133, 137; red-brown, no. 19
Bufo marinus, 109, **174**
Buga, Colombia, 121
burials, 27, 142-44, *147, 171,* 182, 192-95, 197; secondary, **35, 58**
burial urns, **35, 36, 58,** 78, 82, 142, *142;* no. 14; *see also* funerary vessels
butterfly motif, 68, 104, 108, **119, 132,** *189, 198;* nos. 154-55

caciques, 173-78, 182, 193, 194, 197
Caicedonia, 132
Cali, **128,** 135, 152
Calima region, 13, 15, *26,* 31-32, **35, 44,** 50, 61, **63,** 78, **81,** 86, 95, 96, 100, **103,** 104-8, 109, 127, 135, **140,** 144, 148, *148,* **151,** 152, 153, 154, **163, 167;** nos. 21, 37, 41, 43, 45, 79-80, 101-2, 110, 112, 118, 121,

126-27, 129-31, 144, 160; *for specific styles, see* llama style; Yotoco style; Sonso style
canasteros, 26, *26,* 31, 50, 61, **68,** 86, **103, 128,** 147, 149; nos. 19-21, 45, 79
Capulí style, 15, 49, 61, 78, **109, 174, 189, 195;** no. 87
Caribbean Lowland region, 15, 168, *171;* nos. 31, 46, 82; Zenú ceramics, 163-203
Cauca River, 17, 122, 126, 153
Cauca Valley region, 15, 19, 31-32, **32,** 50, 78, **82,** 100, 121, 126, 127, *132,* 132, 135, **144,** 148, 153, **167,** 172, 173, 178-82; *see also* Late llama style; Malagana chiefdom; Malagana style; Middle Cauca region
cayman, *see* crocodilian (cayman) motif
Central America, 19, 22, 67, **95**
chairs, funerary, **53,** 57; no. 28
chanting figures, **108, 115;** nos. 87, 89
Chavín Culture, 44
chevrons, 96, **151**
chicha, 197
chieftain jars, 86, 87-93
chieftains, see *caciques;* rulers
chilam, 48
Chilam Balam, 48
Chile, **116, 119**
Chimila style, 15, **121, 131, 132;** nos. 105, 107; related style, no. 59
Chiminigagua, 86
Choco region, 44-48
Chorrera style, *153,* 154
coca leaf, **25,** 36, 40, 48, 50, 95, **96, 104, 154**
Colombian Institute of Anthropology, 126
color, gender-coded, 21, **147, 167, 198**
companion figures, 26, 36, 49, 50; nos. 35, 51
composite figures, **144**
Contractors Ltd., 53
coqueros, 50
Cordilleras, 17; Central, 17, 126; Eastern, 17, 18, 86; Western, 17, 31, 122, 127, 144, 152, 153
corn, 197
Costa Rica, 43, **167**
crab motif, **182;** no. 148
cream-colored pottery, 171; nos. 18, 50, 100; cream-brown, no. 82
crocodilian (cayman) motif, 44, 48, **49,** 68, **87,** 104, 108, 109-10, 115, 147,

149, **164, 167, 190, 191**
crosshatching, **35, 103**
cross-in-lozenge design, 149
crowns, **44,** 86, **115,** 149, 152
cubist style, 36, **74**
Cuna Indians, 149, 186
cups with covers, *182,* 195

Darién, 192; goldwork, **95**
death, Indian view, 18-19
deer motif, 104, 108, 116, **201;** no. 167
deities, 22, 100, **151, 171;** female, **57,**
    58, 61, **61, 73;** *see also* solar deity
diadems, *152,* 153, 154, 182, 197, 201
dignitaries: reclining, **47;** seated, 26,
    27, 39, 40, 43, 48-49; nos. 8-9, 13, 23
Dominican Republic, *67*
dots, **35,** 104, **159, 178**
dragon motif, **35,** 43-44, 48, 68, **88,**
    164, 171
drum, no. 94; figure playing, no. 91
duality, theme of, **31,** 43, 44, **92,** 100,
    108-9, **147, 159, 168**

eagle motif, 44, 48, 87-92, 108, **186;**
    nos. 27, 153
ear ornaments, **132,** 154, *172,* 182,
    182, *194,* 201; nos. 66, 150, 152;
    earrings, no. 80; earspools, 21, 43,
    152, 153, 154, 192; no. 10
Ecuador, 18, 22, 31, 32, 49, 53, **151,**
    152, 153, *153,* 154
El Dorado: The Gold of Ancient Colombia
    exhibition (1974), 7, 11, 13
emanations, see *tingunas*
Embera Indians, 44-48, 197, 198
emeralds, **81,** 153
Esmeraldas, 152
eyes: avian, **96;** coffee-bean shaped,
    67, 74, 131, 135; moveable, **160**

"Fabulous Beast," 147
face, 21; at chest, **82;** and masks,
    93-95; wrinkled, 96-100, **151, 159**
Falchetti, Ana María, 19, 163-203
Faraquiel, 193
feathered helmet, no. 22
feline motif, **71, 78, 93,** 100, 104, 108,
    116, 144, 147, **159, 164, 167, 178,**
    197, 198, **201;** nos. 76, 132-33, 151,
    161, 167; *see also* jaguar motif
female deities, **57,** 58, **61, 73**
female figures, 49, 50, *172,* 178-92,
    197; with child, 61-67, **67, 68,** 192;
    nos. 40, 44-45; dignitaries, **27, 73, 77;**
    nos. 33, 38, 55; kneeling, 132, 140,
    149, *172,* **178,** 182; nos. 38, 41, 82;

pregnant, **27, 81, 108;** seated, 26-27,
    27, 32, 36-40, 48, 50, 182; nos. 6, 18,
    31, 33-34, 36, 40, 86-87; standing,
    26, 57-58; nos. 46-52, 55, 64
female form: bowl, no. 109; jars, *140;*
    no. 103
female gender associations, 73, 149;
    colors, **147, 167**
fertility, 35, 44, **71, 119, 147, 189**
figure-pendant, *132*
Finzenú, *171,* 173-78, 193, 194
fist, clenched, **140**
flutes, **87, 110, 115,** 202; no. 65
Fondo de Promoción de la Cultura,
    Santafé de Bogotá, 12-13
Forero, Eduardo, 126
frog motif, 78, 104, 108, 109, **174,**
    191, 195
funerary chairs, **53,** 57; no. 28
funerary vessels, 194-95, 197; urns, **35,**
    40, 93, 193, 202-3; nos. 11, 34, 97,
    99, 107; *see also* burial urns

gender-based differences, 21, 26, 32,
    73, 149; colors, **147, 167, 198**
geometric decoration, **73, 77, 92, 116,**
    119, 171, **201;** *see also* triangles
gold and goldwork, 7, 43-44, **50,** 61,
    68-73, 93, **95,** 100, *110,* 122, 127,
    128, 132, 132-35, 140, 142, 143, *148,*
    149, 149-52, *152,* 153-54, **160,** 173,
    186-92, *194,* 194, 201; nos. 3-5,
    10, 22-23, 25, 27, 30, 43, 58, 60-63,
    66-72, 77, 83, 85, 90, 95, 108,
    127-30, 138, 145, 148, 150, 152-55,
    158, 160, 164
granular-and-incised tradition, *172*
Guane Indians, 18, 48, 86
Gulf of Urabá region, 13, 15, 26-27, **40,**
    192; nos. 10, 18, 30, 50

hands: in cubist style, 36; of female
    figures, 32, 57-58; on knees, 22, 26,
    27, 32, 48; at navel, 57, 58-61, **74, 77**
head: with concave depression on top, 58,
    71; with flat top, **61;** trapezoidal, **74**
head and feet elements, no. 117
headband, *128,* 132-35
headdresses, 43; radiating, **35,** 92; *see*
    also crowns; diadems
helmet, feathered, no. 22
Herrera, Leonor, 19, 121-54
Herrera style, 15
Highland Nariño region, 13, 15, 26,
    49-50, 61, 95, 104, 108, **109,** 116,
    151, 154, **174, 189, 195;** nos. 87,
    94, 96, 122-23, 156, 162, 165-67;

for particular styles, see Capulí style;
    Piartal style; Tuza style
Hopi, 18
house-shaped vessels, *135,* 140; no. 119
Huehueteotl, 100, 104
Humboldt, Baron Alexander von, 121

Ika, **25**
llama style, 15, *26,* 31, **44,** 50, **58,** 61,
    63, 68, 73, 86, 95, 96, 100, **103,** 108,
    109, 126, 127, **128,** 144-48, *148,*
    149, 153, **159, 160, 163;** nos. 21, 37,
    41, 45, 79-80, 101, 110, 112, 118,
    121, 126, 128, 131, 144; Late, 15,
    43-44, 100; nos. 58, 61-62, 66-67,
    70-71, 85, 129-30, 148, 152
Inca, 18, 49
incense burner lid, no. 142
incised decoration, **81, 96, 164,**
    167, 195; *see also* Betancí
    modeled-and-incised style
Institute for Scientific Studies in the
    Department of Valle del Cauca, 126
Intermediate Area, 22

jaguar motif, 44, 48, 68, **71, 88, 96,**
    100, 104, 108, **164,** *186,* 197, **197**
Janus-style figures, **163**
jars, 43, 48-49, **53,** 78, 82-86, **125,**
    128, 131, 178; nos. 24, 54, 64, 100-
    103, 105-6, 110, 131, 144, 151, 157;
    chieftain, 86, 87-93; no. 106;
    whistling, *127,* 132, 153
Jones, Julie, 7-8

Kalima, 44
kneeling figures, 73, **103,** 132, 140,
    149, 178, 182; nos. 38, 41-42, 82
knees: clasped or held, **104, 119,** 149;
    hands on, 22, 26, 27, 32, 48
Kogi Indians, 18, **25, 35,** 43, 92, 93,
    104, **186, 189, 197**

Labbé, Armand, 9-10, 15, 17-19, 21-119
labrets (lip plugs), 21, 43, **48,** 82, 87;
    no. 25
La Guajira, 17, **190;** *see also* Baja
    Guajira
Lake Guatavita, 53, 57, 132
Lake Iquaque, 86
La Tolita culture, 32, 152; *see also*
    Tumaco-La Tolita style
lids, 40; nos. 140, 142
ligatures, **39, 58**
lime flasks *(poporos),* 25, 32-36, 40,
    149, *149,* 152; no. 5
lip plugs, *see* labrets

Loma de Segovia, 96
Lord of Fire, 100, 104, *151*

Magdalena, Department of, 15, 40; nos.
 59, 105, 107
Magdalena River, 17, 153; Lower region,
 15, **27**, **35**, **36**, 40, 50, 172, 182, 186,
 202; nos. 11, 34, 48, 65, 99, 125,
 145; Middle region, 15, **36**, 40, 50,
 53, 57, 78, **95**, **121**; nos. 14, 28, 68-
 69, 88, 97, 138, 150; Upper region,
 40, 135
Malagana chiefdom (complex) and
 cemetery finds, *121-54, 122, 127,
 132, 135, 142, 143, 144,* **144,** *147,
 149, 152, 153*
Malagana style, 8, 13, 15, 19, **21**, 31,
 32, **32**, **35**, **43**, 43-44, **63**, 73, 78, **81**,
 82, 86, **99**, 100, **108**, **110**, **115**, 126,
 126, 127, 128, *128, 132,* 132-35,
 140, 140-44, **144**, 148-49, 152, 153,
 154, **160**, *182*; nos. 1, 19-20, 42,
 57-58, 61-62, 66-67, 70-71, 76, 81,
 85, 89, 91, 93, 115-16, 119, 128,
 148, 152
Malamboid style, 15, 44, 108, 109-15,
 164, **167**, **191**; nos. 132-33, 136-37,
 159
Malambo style, 15; no. 125
male figures: with child, 50, 61, 67;
 no. 39; reclining, no. 24; seated, 26,
 27, 32, 36, 50, **58**, **62**; nos. 2, 11,
 35, 37, 39, 79; squatting, no. 84;
 standing, nos. 53, 60, 62-63; *see
 also* priests; shamans
male form, jar, no. 102
male gender associations, 73, 149;
 colors, **147**, **167**, **198**
male nudity, 53, **104**
Malibú-related style, 27, 40; no. 17
Malibú style, 15, **87**, *171,* 172, 186,
 202-3; nos. 29, 65
masks, 8, 93-104, *126,* 132, 142, 143,
 149, **151**, 152, 153, **160**; nos. 120-30;
 figures wearing, **96**; nos. 74, 76, 127
Master of Animals, 116
Maya, 22, 48, **178**
Mayajuez, hacienda of, 128
Mesoamerica, 19, 22, **27**, 44, 100, **151**,
 168
metates, 57; tomb of, 142, *143*
Mexico, 19, **35**, 43, **58**, 95, **99**, **178**
Middle Cauca region, 15, 22, 26, 27,
 32-36, 49, 50, 61, 95, **108**, **115**; nos.
 4, 5, 15, 22, 35, 39-40, 51-52, 64,
 86, 103, 109, 135

Minca, no. 6
minga, 126
Moche culture, 22, **140**
mochila, **96**
modeled-and-painted ceramics,
 172, *172,* 182, *182, 186, 192, 193,*
 194-95, 198, 201
mohanes, 173, 193
monkey motif, 108, **189**; no. 156
Montelibano style, 15, **61**, **178**; nos. 38,
 147
Moseley, Michael Edward, 121
Moskito style, 15, **35**, 40; nos. 11, 34
mother-and-child theme, 61-67, **67**, **68**;
 nos. 40, 44-45
mouth, open, 77, 78, **104**, **108**; no. 162
múcuras, 49, 86-87, **131**; nos. 16, 104
Muisca region and style, 13, 15, 18, 19,
 25, 26, **31**, **39**, 48-49, 50, 53, 73, **81**,
 86-87, **104**, 108, *110,* **119**, **131**, 132,
 139; nos. 3, 8, 16, 23, 32-33, 60, 63,
 83, 104, 113-14
Mundé, **58**
Museo del Oro, Santafé de Bogotá, 7, 8,
 11, 13, 122
musicians, *186,* 197; no. 90

Naguanje style, 15, 108, 109, **168**; no.
 139
Nahuatl-speaking peoples, 95, **168**
Nanahuatzin, 43
Nariño, Department of, 15, 49, 78; *see
 also* Highland Nariño region; Pacific
 Coastal region
navel, hands at, 57, 58-61, **74**, **77**
Nechi River, 36, 173
necklaces, **57**, **61**, **63**, 87, *144, 148,*
 152; nos. 4, 43, 158, 160
North America, 18, 19
Northern Colombia region, nos. 47, 72-73
North Santander, no. 140
nose ornaments, 43, **61**, 87, 104, **132**,
 152, 154, *172,* 186; nos. 108, 154-55,
 164; rings, 21, **167**, *173,* 182, 186,
 197; nos. 86, 138

ocarinas, **32**, **35**, 43, 50, 92, 108, **178**,
 189, **195**; nos. 9, 13, 146, 161
Olmec, 22, 44, **58**
Ometeotl, 100, 104
owl motif, 144, **178**; no. 145

Pacific Coastal region, 15, 31, 32; nos.
 2, 53, 56, 124, 142
painted decoration: figures on bowl, no.
 96; negative, *127,* 148, 152; *see also*
 modeled-and-painted tradition

Palmira, Colombia, 122
Panama, 43, 44, 68, **144**, 186, 192
Panzenú, *171,* 173
parent-with-child theme, 50, 61-67, **62**,
 67, **68**; nos. 39-40, 44-45
Pasto, 116
pectorals, 21, **61**, 100; nos. 68-69, 77,
 127, 145
pedestal vessels, nos. 49, 147, 149
Pelaya style, 15
pendants, 8, 49, **50**, 87-92, *132,* 152,
 153; nos. 23, 30, 58, 62, 70-72, 85;
 avian, **31**, **47**, 49, **96**, **131**; nos. 27,
 153
Peru, 22, **27**, 44, **99**, **140**
phalli, erect, **21**, **81**
Piartal style, 15, 49, **195**, **201**; nos.
 162, 166
pincers in the form of a crab, no. 148
Planeta Rica, 194
Popayán region and style, 8, 15, 53; no.
 92
poporos, see lime flasks
postures, 21, **21**, 22, 73-78, **103**, 149
pottery, meaning of, 198, 202
priests, 18, 22, **25**, 26, **27**, 32, **47**, 53,
 68, **77**, **78**, **81**, 93, **96**, **108**, **110**, **178**,
 194; nos. 59, 61, 72, 74, 76, 78, 85,
 146; *see also* shaman-priests
Proto-llama period, 126-27, 147-48
Pubenza polychrome style, 15, **121**;
 no. 97
Pueblo Indians, 19

Quechuan group, 53
Quimbaya style, 13, 86, 132, 135, 152;
 no. 64; Classic, 15, 22, 36, 50, **74**;
 nos. 4-5, 90, 109; Late, 15, 36, **58**,
 74, 82, **115**; nos. 15, 22, 35, 39-40,
 51-52, 86, 103

rain-making, **77**, 78, 96, **151**
Ranchería style, 15, **168**; nos. 36, 140
rattles, 104, **136**; figures holding, nos.
 59, 90
reclining figures, **47**, 53-57; no. 24
reclining stool, 57, *67*
resist decoration, 49, **62**, **140**, 148
Restrepo, *148*
retablos, 27-31, 36, 50, 61-67, **62**
Rio Bolo, 126
Rio Chiquito, 153
Rio Dagua, 152
Rio Palomino region, **190**
Rodríguez, Carlos Armando, 128
rulers, 22, **25**, 26, 53, 32, **81**, 93; no.
 59; see also *caciques*

San Agustín region, 13, 40, 50, 78, 135, 147, 152, *152,* 153-54
San Andrés de Sotavento reservation, 168, 192-93, 197, *197, 198,* 201, 202
San Jorge River region, 36, 171, 172, 173, *182,* 192, 193, 194-95; Lower region, 15, 40, *168,* 168-71, 172, 178, 202; no. 111; Middle region, 15, 172, *172, 173,* 182, 186; nos. 38, 147
Cardale Schrimpff, Marianne, 19, 121-54
seated figures, 21-22, 26-57, **39, 43, 58,** *110,* 149, 182; nos. 1-3, 6-7, 9, 11-20, 23, 26, 31-37, 39-40, 79, 81, 86-87, 92; shaman, 73-78; no. 83
Sepulcher of the Devil, 194
serpent motif, **27, 31,** 48, 49, **53,** 86-87, **99,** 108, *128,* **164**
shaman-priests, 48, 67, **95, 131**
shamans, 19, 22, **25,** 27, **27,** 44, **53,** 53, 57, 67-78, **77, 78, 88, 92,** 93, **99, 100, 103, 104,** 109, **110, 115,** 116, **119, 186, 189;** nos. 61, 66-67, 72-73, 76, 83, 85, 90-91, 93, 95; animal associations, 44, 48, **57,** 68, 73, 78, **78,** 87, **96, 100,** 104, 116, **119, 164, 178, 182, 189;** no. 93; bench attribute, 27, 32, 44-48, 53, 182; chants and power songs, **36,** 40, 68, 78, **103, 104, 108, 109, 110, 115;** postures, **21, 27,** 57, 73, **103, 104, 119;** shapeshifting and transformations, **50,** 68, **71,** 109, **164, 174, 182, 185, 189,** 197; soul flight, **32, 50,** 68, 73, **88, 92,** 109, **174;** vision, **178, 182**
shells, sheathed with gold foil, 152-53
Sierra Nevada de Santa Marta, 18, **25,** 40, 43, 48, 86, 87
Sinú hat designs, *197, 198,* 201, *202*
Sinú River region, 13, 19, 26, 36, **39,** 49, 50, *61,* **77,** 104, 108, 172, 173, **178,** 192, 194, 197; Lower Sinú, 168, 193; Middle Sinú, 15, **27,** 50, 58, 61, **67,** *186;* nos. 44, 49, 54-55, 149; Upper Sinú, 193
Sinú style, no. 145
snake motif, 147, *198*
solar deity, **27, 35,** 43, 44, **47,** 53, 57, **62,** 86, 87, 92-93, **96, 99,** 100-104, **115, 119, 131, 151, 159, 160, 186**
Sonin, Robert, **88**
Sonsoid period, 121, 126, 128
Sonso style, 15, 31, **128;** no. 102
South America, 19, 67
Southwestern Tradition, 149-52, 154
Spondylus shells, 44, 143
squatting figures, 26, *26,* 31, 73, **103;** nos. 20-21, 80, 84

staff, **25,** 50-53, **57**
staff finials (heads), *61,* 104, 201
standing figures, 57-67; nos. 46-48, 50-53, 55-57, 61-64, 67, 76, 85, 90
star, eight-pointed, 116, **119**
Stemper, David Michael, 126, 128
stools, *67;* figures seated on, **27,** 32
styles, table of, 15
sun, **27, 35, 44,** 57, 110-15, 116, **147;** at night, *182, 185; see also* solar deity

Taino, 41, 57, *67*
Tairona region and styles, 13, 15, 18, **27, 32, 35,** 40-43, 44, **47,** 48, **48,** 50, **50,** 53, 57, 86, 87-92, **96, 100,** 104, **104,** 108, **119, 122, 125, 132, 144, 163, 164, 167, 168, 171, 174, 178, 185, 186, 189, 190, 195, 197;** nos. 100, 141; Early Tairona, nos. 143, 151; Late Tairona, 15, 40-43, 44, 87-93, 109, **191;** nos. 6-7, 9, 12-13, 24-27, 74-75, 77-78, 84, 95, 98, 106, 108, 117, 134, 146, 153-55, 157-58, 161, 163; *see also* Malamboid style; Naguanje style
Tamalameque style, 15, **125;** no. 99
tampers, 193
teeth: bared, **160;** two, 100, **151**
textiles, 19, *178,* 192, *192,* 193, *193, 197, 198,* 198-201
Tierradentro region, 13, 15, 50, 95, 96, 132, 135, **151,** 152, 153, 154; no. 120
tingunas (emanations), **27,** 43, 48, 68, **88**
Tlingit Indians, **27**
toad motif, 104-8, 109, **174,** 198
Tolima region and style, 8, 13, 15, 68-73, **92, 95,** 135, 152, 153, **182;** nos. 28, 68-69, 97, 138, 150; Early, 15; no. 88
tombs, *see* burials; Malagana chiefdom and cemetery finds
Tonatiuh, 43, 100
tongue: distended, **27, 35,** 43, **96, 99;** split or grooved, **31,** 43
tortoise motif, 147, *198*
totuma, 197
triangles, 68, **88, 115, 182**
tropical forest cultures, 67, **104**
Tukano, 73, **73, 104, 119,** 168
Tuluá, Colombia, 132, 135
Tumaco-La Tolita style, 8, 13, 15, **22,** 31, 32, 50, **77,** 78, 86, 95, 96, 108, 109, 147, *149,* 152, **174;** nos. 2, 53, 56, 124, 142
tunjos, **81,** nos. 60-61
tumbaga, 92, 108; no. 111

turtle motif, 44, 115, 148, *198*
Tuza style, 15, 49, 95, 104, 108, 116, **119, 154, 189, 201;** nos. 94, 96, 122-23, 156, 165, 167

Urabá, *see* Gulf of Urabá region
urns, *see* burial urns; funerary vessels

Valle del Cauca, Department of, 15; *see also* Calima region; Cauca Valley region; Popayán region
Venezuela, 44
vessels: anthropomorphic, nos. 17, 114; ceremonial, 194-95; gourd-shaped, no. 88; house-shaped, *135,* 140; no. 119; loop-handled, *178;* pedestal, no. 147; from the tomb of the metates, 140, *143;* zoomorphic, nos. 134, 136, 139, 141, 159, 163; *see also* bottle; bowls; burial urns; cups; jars
village scenes, ceramic, 144; no. 118

whistles, **178, 195;** nos. 74-75, 78, 84; see also *ocarinas*
whistling jars, *127,* 132, 153
winged figures, **32, 88,** 109, **174**

Xiucoatl, **35**

Yotoco style, 15, 31, **81,** 100, 108, 121, 127, **140,** 144, 148, 152, 153; nos. 43, 127, 164
Yucatec Maya, 48

Zenú, 163-203, *171, 172, 182, 192, 193, 197;* goldwork, 15, 171, *172, 173, 173,* 192, 194, *194,* 201; no. 111
Zenufana, *171,* 173, 178, 194
zoomorphic representations, 104-16, 197; nos. 69, 89, 92, 131, 134-37, 139-42, 157, 159, 162-63; *see also* animals